Don't Settle for Your Luck. Do Something About it! LEARN TO BE LUCKY!

If Lady Luck seems to have turned her back on you, don't take it out on her. It may be your fault. Max Gunther has interviewed hundreds of lucky and unlucky people to discover the five secrets that make all the difference. There are five traits lucky people share. Once you know them and have discovered how easy they are to cultivate, you can begin immediately to make luck start working for you.

* Do you know how to take a streak of bad luck and make it start running the other way?
* Have you listened to a piece of Work Ethic advice that's a sure-fire recipe for bad luck?
* Are you holding on to attitudes that are open invitations to misfortune?

Max Gunther reveals the proven methods that have led hundreds of men and women to happiness and success. They were lucky. Now you can be lucky, too!

❈ THE LUCK FACTOR ❈

Why Some People Are Luckier than Others and How You Can Become One of Them

Max Gunther

BALLANTINE BOOKS . NEW YORK

Library of Congress Catalog Card Number: 76-30346

ISBN 0-345-27440-7

This edition published by arrangement with Macmillan Publishing Co., Inc.

Printed in Canada

First Ballantine Books Edition: June 1978

To Dorothy, the best of my luck

Contents

The Quest   ix

PART I. *The Breaks*

1. The Blessed and the Cursed   3
2. Two Lives   20

PART II. *Speculation on the Nature of Luck: Some Scientific Tries*

1. The Randomness Theory   33
2. The Psychic Theories   53
3. The Synchronicity Theory   67

PART III. *Speculations on the Nature of Luck: Some Occult and Mystical Tries*

1. Numbers   87
2. Destiny and God   101
3. Charms, Signs, and Portents   110

PART IV. *The Luck Adjustment*

Introduction   123
1. The Spiderweb Structure   125
2. The Hunching Skill   139
3. "Audentes Fortuna Juvat"   163
4. The Ratchet Effect   182
5. The Pessimism Paradox   195

The Quest

GATHER AROUND ME, ye seekers, and prepare yourselves for a strange journey. We are about to explore a place that few have ever tried to explore before: the territory of luck. It is unexplored mainly because many men and women believe it to be unexplorable, not an area you can make sense of. The word "luck," in this view, is just the name we give to the uncontrolled and uncontrollable events that crash in and out of our lives. It is no more possible to map those events, many would hold, than to map the surf of a wild ocean. To reduce it to order, to measure its fearful geometry: such an undertaking seems bound to fail.

But you will discover, before we reach the end of this quest, that your luck is not as wild a thing as you may have supposed. Within limits, but in a perfectly real way, it can be influenced.

Sense can be made of it.

It can be handled rationally.

To handle it—to improve the odds in favor of good luck and diminish the odds of bad luck—you will need to make some changes, perhaps fairly profound ones, in and around yourself. These changes interlock with and complement each other. Together, they form what I call the *luck adjustment*.

The theory of the luck adjustment is based on observations of consistently lucky as against consistently unlucky people—hundreds of observations, spread over more than two decades. It turns out that the lucky exhibit five major characteristics which, in the unlucky, are either muted to the point of ineffectuality or aren't there at all. We will probe these five traits with care to see what they are made of and how they work. Briefly, they are:

The spiderweb structure. Lucky people use it to create personal channels along which good luck can flow.

The hunching skill. Lucky men and women are aware, instinctively if not consciously, that it is possible to perceive more than you see.

The "audentes fortuna juvat" phenomenon. Typically, the lucky life is lived in a zigzag, not a straight line.

The ratchet effect. It is used instinctively by the lucky to prevent bad luck from becoming worse luck.

The pessimism paradox. The label "happy-go-lucky" is highly misleading, for it doesn't fit most of those whose lives have been objectively lucky. On the contrary, lucky people as a breed cultivate hard, dark pessimism as an essential item of survival equipment.

Each of these five attitudes toward life and self incorporates subsidiary attitudes, corollary rules. Many of these subattitudes surprised and puzzled me when I first became aware of them, and it is likely they will surprise you too. For instance, you will learn that many hoary old pieces of Work Ethic advice are, in fact, recipes for bad luck. And that a single word, "rash," can do you a lot of damage if you let it. And that a cherished superstition, if you have one, may not only be harmless but may even be tangibly useful. And that . . .

But we will get there when the time comes. We are now ready to go. Bring your skepticism with you, but also your willingness to listen. Keep your wits about you and your eyes wide open. Good luck.

❁ PART I ❁

The Breaks

1.

The Blessed and the Cursed

SOME PEOPLE ARE luckier than others. That is a statement with which few would argue. But the statement is like thin soup eaten before a meal. By itself it doesn't satisfy. More must follow, and that is when the arguments begin.

Why are some people luckier than others? This is a question of enormous size, for it probes into people's fundamental beliefs about themselves, their lives, and their destinies. There is no agreement on this question, never has been, perhaps never will be. Some think they know the reasons for good and bad luck. Others agree that reasons may exist but doubt they can be known. Still others doubt that there are any reasons at all.

And so the debate begins.

Eric Leek, barber and hair stylist. He has done a lot of thinking about luck in recent months, for luck has blundered into his life and radically altered its course. Anxious to hear his philosophy, I seek him out at his home in North Arlington, New Jersey. I have an

3

address, but it isn't quite adequate. It is the address of a walkup apartment above some stores on an old, decaying street. Next to a drugstore I find a dim, unmarked doorway that I surmise is Eric Leek's address. The dented metal mailbox in the hallway has no name on it. Up a flight of creaky wooden stairs I find another unmarked door. Hoping I have come to the right place, I knock.

Eric Leek lets me in. He is a tall, lean, handsome man of 26, with light-brown hair and mustache. The apartment is old but lovingly maintained. Leek introduces me to his friend, Tillie Caldas, who insists on bringing me a bottle of beer because, she says, it makes her uncomfortable to see a guest sitting with nothing. A third member of the household is a small, friendly, ginger-and-white cat who is introduced to me as Keel—Leek spelled backward. Eric Leek remarks that his entire name spelled backward is Cire Keel, and he says there was a medieval sorcerer of that name. He thinks it possible that he is Cire Keel's reincarnation.

We turn to the subject of luck. "It worries me to talk about luck," says Leek, "because when I do, some people think I'm weird. My views on it are primarily religious—or mystical, if you prefer. I believe good luck comes to people who are ready for it and will use it unselfishly, to help others. I don't believe it often comes to the greedy. As a general rule, the greediest people I know are also the unluckiest."

Leek will have ample opportunity in years ahead to demonstrate his sincerity. On January 27, 1976, this obscure young man abruptly became stunningly wealthy. He won a special Bicentennial Year lottery conducted by the state of New Jersey, and his prize was the richest ever awarded in any lottery in the nation's history—$1,776 a week, or slightly over $92,000 a year, for life. He and his heirs, if he dies unexpectedly early, are guaranteed a total of at least $1.8 million.

His winning ticket, which cost him a dollar, was one

4

of 63 million in the drawing. "I know what the question is," he says. "The question is, why did that one ticket win? Out of all those people, why me? I don't think it was just something that happened at random. There's a reason for everything that happens, even if we can't always see the reason. There are patterns . . . there's something that guides our lives."

He has always been lucky, he says. "I've never done much worrying about the future because, for me, it always seemed to take care of itself. That's one reason why I've never 'settled down,' as the phrase goes." He has been at various times a singer and actor (which shows in his smooth, precise way of talking), a taxi driver, a construction laborer, a barber. "I always had a strong feeling some big change would happen in my life at about this age. I wasn't in any hurry to find myself because I knew something would happen to change everything, and out of that change would come guidance."

"You felt you knew the future?" I ask.

"In a vague way, yes. Tillie and I are both semiclairvoyant."

"That's right," says Tillie. "A few weeks before all this happened, I dreamt I was with a light-haired man who won a fantastic amount of money. It's funny, though: I didn't connect the dream with Eric at first. That came later. Just before the drawing I suddenly found I was sure he would win."

"I got sure at the end too," says Leek. He recalls that the adventure began with no precognitive hint of its outcome. "I didn't really think about the possibility of winning anything. The proceeds from the lottery were earmarked for a state education fund, and I bought tickets because that seemed like a good cause. I bought maybe forty of them over a span of months, whenever I had a spare dollar. The lottery was set up so that forty-five finalists would be picked for the big drawing. One day I read in the newspaper that the finalists' names would be announced the next day, and I said to a friend, 'My name will be on that list.' It was a gag but not a gag, if that makes any sense. I kind of thought it was true. And of course it was."

Then the number 10 entered the story. Leek regards 10 as his lucky number. "I was born on the tenth hour of the tenth day of the tenth month. Most good things that happens to me have a ten in the picture somewhere. I met Tillie on the tenth, for instance." One good omen lay in the date of the final lottery drawing: January 27. The three digits of the date, 127, add up to 10. Another numerical omen turned up during the drawing itself. The drawing was held in a college auditorium with most of the finalists present. It was a theatrical and complicated procedure, studiously protracted to heighten the suspense. At one stage of this long process, Leek's name arrived at a "post position" marked 10. That, he says, was when he knew he would win.

What will he do with the money? His major plan at the moment is to open a youth center in North Arlington, "to help kids in trouble. My good luck, you see, is going to be turned into good luck for some kids I haven't met yet."

Does he feel he will continue to enjoy good luck? So far, so good. He took Tillie to Acapulco not long after the drawing, and a hotel unknowingly assigned him to just the room he might have asked for: 1010. Back in New Jersey a few weeks later, he attended a barbers' union meeting. A lottery was held. Since Leek was locally famous by that time, he was asked to pick the winner's name from an urn held over his head. The name he picked was his own.

Jeanette Mallinson,* unemployed clerk-typist, in her late thirties, slightly overweight but attractive. She has brown hair and blue eyes. We meet at a drugstore lunch counter in Washington, D.C. Next to her coffee cup is

* Pseudonym.

a newspaper in which she has been studying the help-wanted ads.

She says, "I'm always finding myself out of work, it seems." There is no whine in self-pity in her voice, however. On the contrary, she seems unaccountably cheerful. "I read something by a psychologist once, saying people make their own bad luck. But in my case that isn't true—not the whole truth, anyhow. I've had a lot of bad luck in my life, much more than my share, I think. When I say bad luck, I mean things beyond my control. I think it's destiny. Some people are singled out to have bad luck for a time. But it doesn't have to last forever. In my case things will get better next year—and the year after that, at last, everything will go my way."

"How do you know that?"

"My horoscope says so. Maybe that sounds like superstition to you, but listen, when you've had as much hard luck as I have, you begin to wonder what it's all about. I tried religion, but that didn't give me any good answers. Finally a friend got me interested in astrology, and I was amazed by how accurate it is. See, my sun sign is Scorpio, but I've got Saturn and Mars in the wrong places and a lot of other problems. Nearly forty years of problems from the day I was born. But it's nearly over now, so instead of worrying about this year, I'm looking forward to next year. I'll make it through this year somehow. I always have made it through. . . ."

The first piece of notable bad luck she can recall, she says, struck when she was a child in Maryland. Somebody tried to start a picnic fire with gasoline, and in the resulting flare-up her left cheek was badly burned. She has since had the damaged skin replaced by plastic surgery, and the only traces visible today are some tiny scars. "But plastic surgery wasn't all that advanced when I was a kid, and anyway my parents didn't have the money. So I went through my teens with this big, ugly red patch on my cheek. You know how sensitive a teenage girl is. The patch wasn't all that disfiguring, but I thought I was too hideous to be seen. I stayed home by myself, didn't go on dates or anything. I became a hermit. They say character makes luck, but with me it was the other way around. Destiny made my character. That burned cheek made me a loner, too shy to look anybody in the face."

Out of high school, Jeanette moved to Washington and went to work as a government clerk. "All my life, I've never held any job longer than three years. Something would always happen to push me back out in the street. Maybe some of the problems were partly my doing, but—well, take my very first job. Somebody stole a bunch of money from petty cash. Who did they accuse? Me, of course. It was just my bad luck that somebody had seen me coming back to the office after hours. I came back to get some shampoo I'd bought and left in my desk drawer, but it looked like I was sneaking in to steal the lousy money. That's how it goes with me. Or take my last job, the reason I'm looking at these help-wanted ads right now. I was going along fine in that job, when what happens? The office manager quits, and the new person they moved in is a real witch of a woman. Nobody likes her and she doesn't like anybody, but for some reason she makes me her main target. I don't know why. I've gone over it and over it in my mind, and I honestly can't think of anything I said or did to make an enemy of her. It was just one of those things, two personalities that struck sparks, plain bad luck. Anyway, she made things so unbearable for me that it was either quit or land in a mental hospital."

There have been several relationships with men and all have turned out badly. She was married at age 22. After three years her husband deserted her, leaving her with two small boys. In her late twenties she met another man named Gene. He seemed, she says, "just right . . . a perfect relationship." He was charmed

8

rather than put off by her two sons and wanted to marry her. A week before the scheduled wedding her mother became seriously ill, and Jeanette had to postpone all her plans and take care of the older woman for several months. It eventually became clear that the mother was going to be an invalid for the rest of her life and would need to live with Jeanette or in a nursing home. The prospect of living with Jeanette's mother or footing nursing-home bills seemed to dampen Gene's enthusiasm. Jeanette talked with him about the problem for several weeks and helped prop up his sagging enthusiasm. He began to talk about rescheduling the wedding. Then another blow fell. One of Jeanette's sons collapsed in school. He turned out to be an epileptic. The epilepsy was a kind that is difficult to treat, requiring frequent visits to a doctor and costly medication. Gene silently vanished.

"My other son has asthma," says Jeanette matter-of-factly, as though that fact should follow obviously and inexorably. "Right now I'm about six months behind in my doctor and drug bills and two months behind in my apartment rent. I had a TV set but it was repossessed last month. . . ."

She sighs. "Well, some people get the breaks and some don't. All you can do is wait out the bad time. If the stars are wrong for you, there's no way you're going to fight it."

Sherlock Feldman, professional gambler. Until his recent death, Feldman was a dedicated student of luck—or, more accurately, of other people's theories about it—and an enthusiastic chronicler of luck's oddballs. He was casino manager at the Dunes, one of the better-known gambling clubs in Las Vegas. He spent his days and nights, mostly nights, watching people play with the distilled essence of luck—people who would rather gamble than sleep.

Everything about Sherlock Feldman was big: his belly, his nose, his black-rimmed glasses, his grin, his lust for life. His tolerance was big too. He listened with patience and sympathy to everybody else's views of luck and absorbed all the theories—and, when he saw fit to propose a theory of his own, proposed it softly.

"You ask me what luck is," he told me once, "and I'll have to say I don't know. People come in here with four-leaf clovers, astrology charts, lucky numbers. They want to control their luck with these gimmicks. Maybe lucky numbers do work for some people, and maybe that's a definition of luck. Luck is being the kind of person lucky numbers work for. But with me, luck has never been anything but things happening in a random way."

Feldman had strange stories to tell, however—stories that, as he freely admitted, he couldn't explain adequately. Some of his favorites had to do with what he called "born losers." He acknowledged that this phrase seemed to contradict his own philosophy. "If luck is random, we should all get roughly equal shares of good and bad breaks. There shouldn't *be* born losers, not if you're talking about pure random luck, like at the roulette table. But there are people who win often, and there are people who break even over the long run, and there are people who never, never win. Why? You tell me if you ever find out."

Feldman was drifting around the casino one night when his observant eye was drawn to a man who didn't seem to belong there. "He was a little guy, maybe forty-five, fifty, with a sad look on his face. He was wearing a sportshirt but he kept putting his hand up to his neck, like he was more used to wearing a tie. He was just standing around all by himself, watching a crowd of people play roulette. I went over to say hello. I didn't think he was planning to rob the place or anything, but in this business you've got to be curious about people, you know?"

The man seemed pleased that somebody wanted to talk to him. He and Feldman chatted for a while. He said he was "in haberdashery" in a small Midwestern town. He and his wife were touring the Southwest on a two-week vacation. His wife had gone to a show with a friend that night and he was by himself. "I thought I'd stop in here and look around," he said. "I'd never be able to show my face back home if people found out I'd been in Las Vegas without seeing a casino."

"There's room to squeeze in at the table if you want to try your luck," said Feldman.

"Oh, my goodness, no. I don't need to try my luck because I already know it's bad. I've never won anything in my life, not even a coin toss. I'm a sure loser."

Feldman nodded amiably and started to walk off. Just then the sad man noticed that somebody had dropped a five-dollar bill under the table. He leaned through the crowd and shouted to the croupier, "There's a five on the floor!"

Amid the noise and confusion the croupier misunderstood. He thought the haberdasher was calling a bet: "Five on four." Accordingly the croupier put a $5 chip on the number 4. The wheel spun. The little ivory ball fell into the "4" slot. The haberdasher's chip had won $175.

The croupier pushed the stack of chips across the table. Stunned, the sad man left the stack where it happened to lie: on the square marked "red." The wheel spun again. Red won. The $175 doubled to $350.

Feldman had picked up the $5 bill from the floor and returned it to a woman player who had dropped it. Now he clapped the haberdasher on the back and said, "Seems to me your luck isn't so bad after all."

"I can't believe it!" said the sad man. "Nothing like this ever happened to me before. I never win. If there's a fifty-fifty chance of losing some game, with me it's a hundred-percent chance. Why, when I used to play poker with the boys back home, they called me Old Cash Flow because I was always sure to subsidize the game."

"Well, tonight's your night," said Feldman. "Looks like your luck has turned at last. Why not let it run?"

The haberdasher did. He went on winning. Eventually his pile of chips totaled more than $5,000, and the tension was more than he could bear. He decided to take the cash and go.

But bad luck was still dogging him in its own mysterious way.

Gaming houses in Las Vegas, as all over the world, often seem charmingly casual in their methods of handling bets and extending credit. But beneath the easygoing surface there are rules of iron. One of the more firmly enforced rules—no exceptions are permitted, ever—has to do with the process of calling a bet. A player may call a bet without actually putting up cash, and if the dealer likes his looks, the dealer will advance him a chip or two and invite him into the game. Eventually, however, the player must produce cash to pay for those opening-stake chips. Even if he wins, he must show that he had enough cash in his pocket to cover the original stake. If he can't show the required amount of cash, the house will apologetically but immovably refuse to cash his winnings for him.

In the haberdasher's case, he had been advanced a $5 chip. The requirement seemed easy enough. To get his $5,000-plus in cash, all he needed to do was show that he had $5 in his pocket.

He pulled out his wallet and looked inside. His smile changed to a look of shock, then of sorrowful surmise. His wife had taken all his cash for her evening's expenses and had forgotten to tell him. The wallet was empty.

We probably should stop now and try to clarify what we mean by "luck." It is a short and charmingly simple word, but one loaded with emotional, philosophical, religious and mystical paraphernalia. There are dozens of possible definitions of this burdened little word. Each definition implies a certain way of looking at life, and each, if you insist on it loudly enough, will get you into fights with other men and women who see life differently and so favor different definitions.

Dictionaries are only of limited help in this quandary. Each dictionary definition can be argued with, for each seems to slight one philosophy or another. Funk and Wagnall's begins by saying luck is "that which happens by chance." Some would call that a fine and complete definition, but others would say no, luck is more than chance. The Random House Dictionary gets off to a more mystical start: "The force that seems to operate for good or ill in a person's life." Force? What force? As for old Noah Webster: "a purposeless, unpredictable, and uncontrollable force that shapes events favorably or unfavorably for an individual, group, or cause." But the devoutly religious would say no, not purposeless. Astrologers and psychic-phenomena enthusiasts would say no, not unpredictable. And many Las Vegas and Monte Carlo and racetrack gamblers would say no, not necessarily uncontrollable either.

I've looked for a definition that everyone can accept—one that simply states the facts and leaves the explanations and analyses behind. And so:

Luck: events that influence your life and are seemingly beyond your control.

That is a broad definition, and it is meant to be. It should satisfy those who believe luck is simply the ebb and flow of random events. And those who, though they feel it is more than just randomness, are convinced the forces can be explained in rational, scientific terms. And those who believe luck involves occult or other-worldly forces: the stars, numbers, spells, rabbits' feet, four-leaf clovers, God.

Each person's definition of luck depends on what his or her life has been like. There is no sense in arguing about somebody else's view of luck, any more than there is in arguing about somebody else's life story. This book will not argue with anybody. We will talk to men and women who hold diverse beliefs and we will listen to their stories and explanations, and when it seems useful, we will investigate what seem to be flaws in logic—but very, very gently and with the utmost humility. We want only to see what men and women do and think about luck. In the course of this quest, we are going to meet many strange philosophies and many strange and appealing people.

Our ultimate purpose is to find out whether there are tangible differences between the consistently lucky and the unlucky. Are there certain things that lucky people do more often than unlucky people? Do the lucky people take certain approaches to life, have certain ways of thinking and acting? Are these things learnable? Can you meld them with your own philosophy of luck, whether that philosophy is stodgily pragmatic or wildly occult or somewhere in between?

The answer to all those questions is yes.

"Shallow men believe in luck," said Ralph Waldo Emerson a century ago. His definition of luck was obviously a narrow one. In making that sour statement he referred to luck in its mystical or metaphysical sense: a nonrandom thing, a force or agency or pattern that pushes people around in mysterious but somehow ordered ways.

But if we apply Emerson's words to our broader definition of luck—events that influence our lives and are seemingly beyond our control—the statement makes no sense. To talk about believing or not believing in luck, as thus defined, is like talking about believing or not believing in the sun. The sun is plainly there, and so is luck. *Everybody's* life is influenced by events that come blundering into it from outside. No man, woman or child can be said to be in total control of his or her own life. We are all subject to the unforeseeable, the unexpected, the uninvited. Sometimes our luck is good and somtimes bad, but it is always an element to contend with. It plays a role in everybody's life, often the commanding role.

It is scary to consider the role played by luck in the

very start of your life. I exist today because, many years ago in London, a young man happened to catch a cold. He worked for a bank in the city. On Sundays, when the weather was good, he liked to go into the country for picnics or down to one of the English Channel beaches for a swim. One spring Sunday, laid low by a cold, he called off his picnicking plans and stayed home in his grubby little furnished room near the bank. A friend dropped in and invited him to a party, where he met a young woman. They fell in love and got married. They were my mother and father.

About a quarter-century after that, another young woman arrived in New York, job-hunting. One prospective job that attracted her greatly was in the personnel department of a university. After being interviewed for the job she waited for a week or so, heard no word, grew nervous about her diminishing cash supply, and reluctantly accepted another, less attractive job offered by a magazine. A few days later the university offered her the job she had really wanted. The offer had been delayed, it turned out, by a series of clerical complications and other trivial events, including the fact that some key decision-maker had been home in bed with the flu. The young woman thought about it for a day, and finally, guided partly by a sense of moral obligation and partly by comfortable inertia, decided to stick with the magazine job she had started. Not much later I drifted around to the same magazine and was hired to work at the rewrite desk. The young woman and I met, fell in love and got married. Our three children would not exist today if an obscure university executive hadn't caught the flu at just the right time.

And so it goes. You can talk about such stories in terms of Fate or Destiny, portentously capitalized, or you can say (as I personally prefer to say) that the stories illustrate nothing but the patternless workings of random events. Either interpretation fits under our broad definition of luck. If we think we exert rigorous, detailed control over our lives through personal planning and direction, we are victims of an illusion.

Many men and women of strong intellect are frustrated and baffled, as Emerson was, by the existence of luck. For luck is the supreme insult to human reason. You can't ignore it, yet you can't plan for it. You can only wait around and know that it will come into your life again and again and again. You cannot know what form it will take or whether its visit will leave you sad or happy or angry, richer or poorer, up or down or somewhere in between.

You cannot know, indeed, whether it will leave you alive or dead.

The human intellect is always trying to make order. Luck is always making chaos. No matter with what care and cleverness you plan your life, luck will surely change the design. With good luck, any half-baked plan will get you somewhere. With bad luck, no plan will work. This is the frustrating characteristic of luck. It is the element that must be, yet can't be, taken into our plans.

All our earnest efforts at self-improvement become virtually futile unless accompanied by the right breaks. You can have courage and perserverance and every other trait admired by the Protestant Ethic, and you can have love and humility and all the traits admired by poets, but unless you also have good luck (as Jeanette Mallinson would tell you), none of it does you much good. You can study personal tactics, like Machiavelli. You can learn techniques for getting power. You can learn to intimidate people, lead them, say no to them without feeling guilty, charm them, hypnotize them, sell them hot-water bottles on the Equator. Or you can go in the opposite direction and learn to be happy inside yourself, learn to pray, learn to meditate, find inner peace, find oneness with God and the Universe. No matter. Any self-enlargement technique that attracts you can probably be made to work for you, but there is an element that must be present if the technique is to work well. It is an element that is seldom acknowledged in the instructions. It is luck. Almost any approach to success and self-fulfillment can work—when you are lucky.

An IBM man of my acquaintance went into a toilet in his office building one day to practice transcendental meditation. The toilet was the only place where he could find the needed solitude. As he began reciting his mantra a loose tile fell from the ceiling and hit him on the head. He leaped up, startled. His car keys fell from his rear pocket and into the toilet. He leaned down to fish them out. In his bewildered state he failed to lean with proper care and leaned on the flush handle. His keys went.

Nothing, *nothing* works without good luck. It would be nice if we could learn to control this enormously powerful element better than most of us do. It would be nice if there were techniques for managing luck as there are for managing everything else.

There have been many attempts to find such techniques. Ever since the earliest tribesmen asked their gods for rain or good hunting or other blessings, most religions have been, at least in part, attempts to control luck. People still pray for favorable outcomes today, carry St. Christopher medals to ward off travel accidents, seek spiritual guidance in choosing between alternatives. Nearly all occult arts similarly try to control the uncontrollable—or, as in astrology, to prepare for it by predicting what kind of luck is on the way.

The very existence of the snobbish word "superstition," however, demonstrates that people can't agree on the unseen forces that may or may not operate in our lives. The word is defined as "any religious, mystical, or occult belief not held by me." What is superstition to me may be religion to you, and vice versa. The trouble with all such approaches is that their efficacy in improving ones' luck has not been demonstrated to everybody's satisfaction. Some may work for some people, but not everybody is willing to try them.

It would be useful if there were approaches to luck control that didn't depend on unseen forces—approaches whose efficacy could be demonstrated in a pragmatic way. There are.

I have been a fascinated collector of luck stories and luck theories since the middle 1950s, when a thunderbolt of good fortune came crashing into my life from nowhere (or so it seemed at the time) and radically altered the design. Since then, in the course of interviewing several thousand men and women for sundry journalistic purposes, I've also interviewed them about luck: their experiences with it, thoughts about it, attempts to control it. I've paid special attention to spectacularly lucky people and also to the spectacularly unlucky. I've asked: What do the luck-blessed do that other people don't do—and particularly that the luck-cursed don't do? Is it possible to change one's luck by making practical changes within or around oneself?

Yes, it is possible, and that is what this book is about. When you know how to do it, you can exert limited but perfectly real control over your luck. You may not be able to control it in the deliberate and detailed fashion envisioned by some mystical and occult practioners—although I will introduce you to many who believe otherwise. Nonetheless, with or without unseen forces to help you, you can position yourself in such a way that your chances of stumbling into good luck and avoiding bad luck are appreciably increased.

For it turns out that there are perceptible differences between the consistently lucky and the unlucky. In general, and with exceptions, the luckiest men and women are those who have adopted certain approaches to life and have mastered certain kinds of internal psychological manipulations. I call this array of traits and attitudes the Luck Adjustment.

I have made this adjustment in and around myself. It produces pleasant results. My friends call me lucky, and it's true: I am. But I believe I'm lucky not just because I'm lucky, but partly because I know how to be.

If my luck and yours both hold for a while, by the time we reach the end of the book, the Luck Adjustment will be making itself useful to you.

We have a fascinating journey ahead of us. We will begin by exploring the realm of luck and finding what various kinds of people do and say and think about it. Gambling deals with luck in its plainest and most direct form, and thus we will study the lives and luck of gamblers to see what truths are to be found there. We will also talk to stock-market speculators and others who challenge raw luck in their daily lives. And we will talk to ordinary, obscure men and women who don't consider themselves gamblers but who actually are, like everybody else.

So come with me, keep your fingers crossed, and kiss your lucky charms. We are about to venture into some strange lands. We will see things that will strain our capacity to understand or believe, and it may be we will come back home with more questions raised than have been answered. Still, we may return a little wiser than we left—if we are lucky.

2.

Two Lives

Issur Danielovitch and Charlie Williams* were born during the First World War in the grimy east end of Amsterdam, New York. They were born with apparently equal chances to succeed or fail. Both their fathers were immigrant laborers, and both families lived on the edge of poverty. The two boys grew up in the same world, were dragged and battered and washed by the same great social tides. They were in grade school during the Roaring Twenties. They were slammed down as teenagers by the Great Depression. They were sucked into the vortex of the Second World War as young men, then spewed out into a peacetime boom. They grew older as America changed through the self-satisfied fifties, the strident sixties, the prudent seventies.

And now they are middle-aged men. They were created equal, but they have not ended equal.

Charlie Williams is known to his friends today as Banana Nose. He is a Bowery bum. Issur Danielovitch

---

* Pseudonym.

is known as Kirk Douglas. He is a Hollywood star and a millionaire.

It will be instructive to analyze the parallel stories of these two men. Heraclitus remarked some 25 centuries ago that character is destiny, and several million plays and novels since then have tried to prove the point. They have not proved it because it is only part of a truth. Character does indeed make destiny, but destiny also makes character. A man's or woman's route through life is determined partly by what is inside: the degree of courage, the oomph, the fortitude, the fervor of hope and dream. But that stuff inside is shaped partly if not wholly by events and other personalities impinging from outside.

Kirk Douglas and Charlie Williams are where they are today partly because of what they are and partly because of events seemingly beyond their control. These are two stories of character and luck intertwined.

I first met Charlie Williams in 1968. A magazine had assigned me to write an article about luck. I went to New York's Bowery district, a place so monumentally ugly that it has an odd, surrealistic charm all its own, and walked into the ill-named Majestic Bar. A dozen ragged, crumpled-looking men were drinking wine there at 15 cents a glass. Most of them were in their fifties or older, which was to be expected. The Bowery is a place where losers end. The human spirit is tough, and it takes years of pummeling to make a loser.

I was barely inside the Majestic's door before a couple of the men slid off their barstools and tried to touch me for dimes and quarters. The bartender growled, "Hey, you guys, no panhandling in here! Go out and do your bumming on the sidewalk!" I told him it was all right, I wanted to buy drinks for the house. This caused a stir along the bar. When I had everybody's attention I explained that I was a journalist, I was writing something about luck, and I wanted to find a man who had been born in the same town and the same year as somebody rich and famous.

This seemed to buffalo them. Those who weren't too drunk to think were racking their brains hard. They could undoubtedly smell my money. "I was on a train with Roosevelt once!" one man shouted hopefully. Another said something about his wife's mother and Senator Taft. Then I found a small man standing next to me. "How about Kirk Douglas?" he said.

The man had an ugly but pleasant face. The nose was much too big for the rest of his features, but so was the grin. His clothes were old but neat, with a faded look that suggested frequent laundering. One shoe was bound with electrician's tape to keep the sole from flapping. He was clean-shaven. His thin brown hair was carefully combed, and his fingernails were clipped short and perfectly clean. He was evidently a man who clung to self-respect despite having ended on life's discard pile.

I bought him a couple of sandwiches and listened to his story.

Charlie Williams was born in 1917, one year before Kirk Douglas. He recalls that he enjoyed his early years in Amsterdam. He did well in school, particularly in mathematics.

Then came the first notable piece of bad luck Wilson can recall. When he was 12 his father happened to hear of a semi-skilled job in Providence, Rhode Island. The family migrated. "It seemed like good luck for my old man because his wages went up a bit, but it was lousy luck for me. I'd been happy in school before, but somehow I never made it in the Providence schools. I ran into some bad teachers. . . ."

There was one who made unkind remarks about his nose, which was growing larger as his young bones matured. The shapes of one's facial and bodily features, of course, are factors over which one has little or no control and which can profoundly affect one's life. Handsome men and beautiful women may not have an automatic edge over their plainer peers, but they do have something that can be turned to personal profit if they use it well. One's face is partly responsible for one's fortune.

Charlie Williams somehow lost his hold on optimism during his teens. "That lousy teacher would say things like, 'What's the matter, Charlie, couldn't read your homework? Nose get in your way?' The kids took it up from her, and I never got to be anything but an outsider. I was Charlie the Beak, the kid everybody laughed at. Well, hell, that bothers a kid. My grades fell. I guess I had—whaddya call it—the loser psychology. I'd only just started, but I was already finished."

He hated school and dropped out. He worked on a farm, then joined a railroad track-repair crew, then drove a school bus. "Every now and then I'd try to get a better job, but I must have had *loser* written all over me. I guess what I did was, I'd apply for a job believing I wasn't going to get it. I'd apologize to the guy for wasting his time. Naturally he wouldn't give me the job."

A woman entered Charlie Williams' life during this period. She moved into his shabby hotel room with him and stayed for a few days. Then she vanished, taking his meager supply of cash. For reasons that were never clear to him, she also took his schoolbus ignition key. Unable to get the bus out on the road next morning, he was fired.

In 1939 a break came Charlie's way. He got a job driving for a small trucking company. He and the owner of the business grew fond of each other. The owner, an older man, wanted to retire but wanted to keep the business alive and providing income. Having no son, he unofficially adopted Charlie. He talked about turning the business over to the younger man as manager and partner. Williams saw a chance to succeed at last. Not for years had he been so enthusiastic about anything. He carefully studied the company's books and the economics of the trucking industry. He made plans to take some courses in accounting. "I was going to be a businessman! I thought, *I've finally made it!* I really thought I had. I liked the business, and knew I was going to be good at it. I was going to make the outfit grow. I was going to be chief of one of them big corporations!"

But destiny had other plans. The United States went to war. One of the very first men invited into the army by the local draft board was Charlie Williams. By the time he returned to civilian life in the middle 1940s, the little trucking business and the owner were both dead.

Charlie drifted from job to job. He had learned to like whiskey in the army, but he was not yet drinking immoderately. A new chance to succeed came his way when the Firestone Tire and Rubber Company hired him in 1948 as a warehouseman. Like many big companies in those days, Firestone had ambitious peacetime expansion plans but was troubled by a postwar lack of young men and women trained in its special technologies. The company's answer was a crash program of employee education. Firestone was continually dipping down into its pool of unskilled workers, lifting them up, sending them to school and channeling them into what, for some, became golden new careers. Charlie Williams, lacking formal education but impressively bright, was one man so lifted. Firestone began by training him as a tire retreader, and there was talk of sending him to night school to complete his high-school education and then perhaps on to a chemical technician's school. "Once more I thought I had it made."

Once more he was wrong. A new piece of bad luck was on the way. One Saturday night he was driving an arthritic 1938 Buick in New Jersey when the steering mechanism gave way. He found the wheel spinning freely in his hands. "I was on a kind of country road. There was only one house anywhere near me. The rest was open fields. The car could have gone in a thousand different directions and I'd have been okay. But what happens? Christ, the car heads straight for the house. You talk about bad luck. Straight for the house, like somebody was steering it. I smash into the side of a garage, and the whole goddamn garage roof collapses."

Charlie wasn't badly hurt, but his career was. He had been drinking that night—but, he steadfastly claimed, not heavily. "I think I had three glasses of beer in me, nothing else." He was charged with drunken driving. Nobody believed his story about the steering mechanism, for the car was too badly smashed to yield supporting evidence. He was uninsured. The owner of the house sued for damages. His Firestone wages were garnisheed.

That ended his bright career at Firestone. He drifted some more. One day in 1950, jobless and hungry, he passed an army recruiting poster. The poster offered several promises that attracted him: a roof, a bed, three square meals a day, the chance to learn new skills. "It seemed like an answer. The way I figured was, you don't get shot at the peacetime army. So a man might as well earn his living there as anyplace else."

He enlisted in this peacetime army on June 15, 1950. Ten days later he discovered that he had made a bad mistake. On June 25, North Korean troops unexpectedly invaded South Korea across the 38th parallel. The U.S. peacetime army abruptly became a wartime army. Within a few months Charlie Williams was in Korea, getting shot at.

"I figured, nothing I ever do is going to turn out right. I figured, from now on the hell with it. Korea is where I started drinking in earnest."

But he had one more resurgence of hope. Out of the army in the late 1950s, he drifted to New York City and started looking for a job. "I was forty, see. I figured I had to make it this time or I'd be through forever. So I quit drinking, dried out completely. I used

25

my army pay to buy a good set of clothes. I mean, I was really determined to give it one more try."

He had no skills to offer any employer, however. And one day, sitting morosely on a park bench scanning help-wanted ads in a newspaper, he had what he now considers the unluckiest break of his entire luckless life. "I'm sitting there and a guy comes from nowhere and sits next to me. A bum, ragged, lushed up. He says, 'Out of a job?' I tell him yes, and he says, 'I'll tell you where to go.' I figure he's going to tell me about some job I can get. Instead, what he tells me— well, it's the end of everything. You might say it's my doom."

The bum told Charlie Williams about New York's Municipal Lodge—"the Muni," its patrons called it— where destitute men could get free meal and bed tickets redeemable at various restaurants and flophouses in the Bowery district. "When I got my free meal and bed that night, I just gave up. The pressure was off. I didn't have to hunt for a job anymore. From that day on I was trapped."

About twice a year after that, Charlie Williams tried to struggle up and out. He held various jobs—washing dishes in a cafeteria, delivering phone orders for a coffee shop, washing cars, stabbing litter in a park— but no job lasted more than a few months. Charlie would get discouraged too easily. If the job produced some series of minor irritations or arguments, he would quit. The pay was always so low that, as he saw it, there was no point in staying when the job became unpleasant. Life had given him no reason to hope that things might improve if he hung on. When each job ended, he would blow his accumulated pay, if any, on red-eye whiskey. Then he would go back to the Muni and spend his days panhandling drinking money on the streets.

I last saw Charlie in 1973. It isn't always easy to find a man who has neither a home, a job, a mailing address, nor a phone, but I made the attempt once in a while and occasionally found him in a bar or lounging on his favorite Broadway corner. I would slip him a few dollars and ask what had been happening to him. Usually nothing had. His life had slowed to a standstill. It was a cold day when I saw him in 1973, and he talked hopefully of bumming his way to Florida. "I'm getting too old for this," he said as the chill November wind blew through his old army overcoat.

Issur Danielovitch was a tough kid in a tough neighborhood. As he expressed it to me many years later, he was "the kind of kid who, as an adult, would end up as a clerk in an Amsterdam department store. I was going no place. I wasn't interested in anything except girls. . . ."

He and Charlie Williams do not recall ever meeting each other. If they had been brought together at about age 11 or 12, however, it is probable that the adults in their world would have picked Williams as the more likely to succeed. Williams was a good student with a special flair for mathematics. Danielovitch was a student who did just enough work to get by and had no apparent interest in any intellectual pursuit.

But to make forecasts about a boy's or girl's future course, and to base those forecasts solely on personality factors observed in the present, is to reckon without what Kirk Douglas calls the "X factor"—luck. Oddly, it seemed to me that Charlie Williams was more comfortable with his bad luck than Douglas with his good luck. By the time I met Williams, he had virtually stopped worrying about it. Douglas, however, remains baffled by many of the things that have happened in his life and spends a good deal of time trying to make sense of them. He admits he can't.

"A man likes to feel he's in control of his life," says Douglas, "but it's a damned illusion. The X factor is always there. You can have all the talent in the world, but without luck you go nowhere."

Among Charlie Williams' first bad breaks were a

series of bad teachers. Issur Danielovitch had precisely the opposite experience. This aimless, girl-crazy kid had the good luck to be assigned to a teacher who was apparently more than good. She was outstanding. Today, as he approaches age sixty, he still remembers that teacher clearly and talks about her often. He credits her with turning his young life around.

"I think she took me on as some kind of project. Maybe she wanted to prove something to herself, I don't know, prove how much you can make out of how little. Anyway, she threw challenges at me, kind of dared me to do things I didn't think I could do. One day she asked me to take a small part in a school play. There was no reason for her to do it. I'd never shown any interest or talent in that direction before. She just did it. It was a fluke. If it hadn't happened, nobody outside Amsterdam would know my name today. But it did happen, and I got interested in acting, and she boosted me and prodded me along, and that's how it started."

Young Danielovitch worked his way through college (partly as a clerk in an Amsterdam department store), then went to New York and tried to break into show business. He met a crowd of other young theatrical hopefuls and had a grand time, but in terms of career advancement he scored close to zero. "I lived in a grubby little room in Greenwich Village, worked as a waiter in a Schrafft's restaurant. I did get a couple of bit parts on Broadway, but they were so small that you could hardly see them without a microscope. One of them actually was invisible, as a matter of fact. I was an offstage echo. This was the kind of success I was having. When I went into the navy in 1942, I seemed to be no further along in my career than when I'd started."

But luck was operating in its own secret way. When Kirk Douglas went off to war, he left behind a large circle of friends. Among the young women he kissed goodbye was an obscure, struggling actress named

Lauren Bacall. While he was out in the Pacific, Lauren Bacall enjoyed an astonishing run of luck and abruptly became a Hollywood star. ("Your own luck depends on other people's luck," says Douglas. "It's crazy!") She induced a producer to watch Douglas act when he returned to civilian life, and thus his movie career began. "Oh, sure," he says, "I guess I had some kind of talent. But if it hadn't been for this Lauren Bacall fluke, where would the talent have gone? Dozens of my friends back then had talent too, but you don't see their names in movies today. They didn't have the luck."

For a while after his arrival in Hollywood, Douglas acted without great distinction in a string of second-rate movies. Then he was presented with two opportunities that seemed more than ordinary. Two production companies approached him within days of each other and offered him major roles. One company was large and wealthy. Its proposed film was to be an expensive one, and the budget included what Douglas thought was a stunningly generous allowance for actors' earnings. The other company was small and far from wealthy. It planned a low-budget film with a bare minimum of guaranteed pay. It could only ask its actors to take their chances. If the film succeeded, they would succeed. If it didn't they would go home with holes in their pockets.

"I chose the little outfit," says Douglas. "Why? I didn't know then and I still don't know today. It was a plain, wild hunch. I've always been a guy who trusts his hunches. When they are strong and feel right, I go with them. This one was very strong, though I couldn't figure out where it came from. I went with it, and it turned out to be right."

The little company's film was *Champion,* a nicely wrought study of the boxing world. This was the movie that made Kirk Douglas a star. The wealthy company's film was received without enthusiasm and vanished into obscurity, along with most of its players.

A hunch like that can be explained rationally, at least in part. In 1958 Douglas had another hunchlike experience that could not be explained rationally. Producer Mike Todd was planning to fly from the West Coast to New York in his private plane and invited Douglas to go with him. Douglas accepted, packed his bags, and didn't go. "I can't explain why I didn't go. There was no feeling of seeing the future, no premonition of disaster or anything like that. At the last moment—well, I just plain decided I didn't want to go. It was one of those decisions you make without knowing the reason." The plane crashed, killing everybody aboard.

Kirk Douglas's life since then has continued to be generally lucky. It has been a life lived largely in public view. It is well enough known so that there is no need to catalog it here.

But the questions remain unanswered. Did Douglas and Williams help make their own luck, and if so, to what extent? Or did their luck come largely from forces beyond them? If that is so, what are those forces and how do they operate?

❃ PART II ❃

*Speculations
on the Nature
of Luck: Some
Scientific Tries*

1.

The Randomness Theory

MARTIN GARDNER, RENOWNED mathematical games-man who writes a monthly column on his topic for the *Scientific American,* is convinced that luck springs from plain randomness. When people talk about "amazing luck" and "winning streaks" and "lucky days," he insists, they are only talking about the coincidences and apparent patternings that are bound to show up when enough random events happen over a long enough time. Mathematician Horace Levinson expresses the same view in *Chance, Luck and Statistics,* one of the few readable books I've ever found on the subject of probability. Another such book is *Lady Luck: The Theory of Probability,* by mathematics professor Warren Weaver, who agrees with Gardner and Dr. Levinson.

Other eminent thinkers disagree, or course. They will have their say, but this chapter belongs to devotees of the randomness theory. Let's see what their theory is and why it makes sense to them.

Some years ago a woman named Vera Nettick, playing bridge at Princeton, New Jersey, picked up a newly dealt hand and nearly dropped it. The hand contained all 13 diamonds.

At first she thought she was a victim of one of those stacked-deck jokes with which bridge players like to torment one another, but she hadn't left the table since the cards were shuffled and finally concluded that this wasn't the case. The dealer, to her right, opened with a bid of two hearts. It was obvious that the other three hands contained long suits and a diamond void, and a bid of seven hearts or spades would have topped hers and might have been makable. She immediately bid a grand slam in diamonds and held her breath. Her opponents elected not to top her, and the grand slam was hers—a laydown. She will undoubtedly talk about that stunning hand for the rest of her bridge-playing life. That night, luck was with her.

Luck? The randomness theory people would disagree. When anybody comes around to them mumbling about "luck" in bridge or any other card game, they point out that every conceivable hand is bound to be dealt to somebody sooner or later. They will even, on request, supply a mathematical calculation by which to estimate how often a hand like Vera Nettick's can be expected to come up. It is more often than most people think.

There are roughly 635 billion possible bridge hands. Of these, eight might be called "perfect" hands, though some are more perfect than others. To begin with, there are four perfect notrump hands. Such a hand would contain all four aces, all four kings, all four queens and one of the four jacks. Any of these four hands would be unequivocally perfect because no bid could top it. Slightly less perfect, in descending order, are hands containing all the spades, all the hearts, all the diamonds, and all the clubs. If there are eight of these perfect hands in a possible 635 billion, the statistical probability is that such a hand will be dealt once in every 79 billion tries, give or take a few.

Now all we have to do is estimate how many games of bridge are played every year and how many hands are dealt in each game. Using fairly conservative estimates, it turns out that a perfect hand should be dealt to some lucky bridge player, somewhere in the United States, roughly once every three or four years.

To the player who picks up that gorgeous hand this year or next year or the year after, the event will seem like monumental luck. To the randomness people it will be utterly unremarkable. (The randomness people are the killjoys of the world of luck.) To them, such an event is as expectable as the rising of the sun. The only difference is that the appearance of a perfect hand is less predictable in terms of time.

Indeed, it would be surprising if perfect hands didn't get dealt occasionally. All the possible hands are equally likely to be dealt. If you specify *any* 13-card hand in advance, the odds against your picking up that particular hand are 635 billion to one. The perfect hand is no more rare than any other. The only difference is that the perfect hand is more wished for, and so is more startling and memorable to the player who gets it, and so gets talked about more. If you are a bridge player, it is unlikely that you can precisely reconstruct the last mediocre hand you played a week ago. You didn't wish for that handful. But if you had picked up a perfect hand, for which the probability is exactly the same, you would remember it and bore your friends with it for decades.

Proponents of the randomness theory will grudgingly grant you the right to be happy if you pick up a perfect bridge hand or win a million-dollar lottery prize, and they will even morosely tolerate your muttering about "luck," but they won't permit you to be surprised. Somebody *must* pick up a perfect hand sooner or later, and if that person happens to be you, you aren't entitled to be astonished. True, the odds against your getting that hand are enormous, but so are the odds against your getting any other group of 13 specific cards. As Dr. Levinson puts it, "The odds are always against what happens."

Dr. Levinson illustrates his point by talking about lotteries. If you enter a state lottery along with a million other people, the odds against your winning the top prize are a million to one. If you do win, Dr. Levinson doesn't want you to be astounded. You will be, of course. You will go around saying "I can't believe it!" and "Why me?" and "Wow, what fantastic luck!" But to the state officials conducting the lottery, nothing at all interesting has happened. One person was *supposed* to win the top prize. From their point of view, the lottery is a reliable machine that does precisely what it was designed to do each time around and generates no surprises. Each time, uncaring, it creates a situation in which one man or woman wins a fortune against staggering odds.

All of life is like that. Things that happen to us seem incredible because the odds against them are so huge, but whatever happens to me was bound to have happened to somebody. If I go out in my car some morning and smash into another car at an intersection, I howl with indignation over my fantastic bad luck. The other driver and I are total strangers who started from different places at different times, are headed toward different destinations for different reasons, have traveled over diverse routes, have had our speed influenced by traffic lights and other drivers (each with his own reasons for being there) and a multitude of other factors. When this hapless day began, the odds against our arriving at this intersection at precisely the same time were colossal: millions to one, billions, trillions. But the police who arrive on the scene are unsurprised. To them, the accident is part of a certainty. They know there are bound to be X-thousand two-car accidents in their state every year. Those accidents must happen to somebody.

What is luck to me is certainty to somebody else. This is one reason why randomness devotees get depressed when people talk about "amazing" strokes of good or bad luck. No true randomness man will every admit to being amazed by anything.

·Not even coincidences surprise these doggedly and often grumpily rational people. They manage to look bored even when outrageously unlikely things happen, even when random events seem to fall together into patterns that have no apparent right to exist. For the randomness theory holds that the laws of probability aren't really all that lawful. There are two cardinal laws to keep in mind. First law: Anything can happen. Second law: If it can happen, it will.

It *will*—sooner or later, given enough random events happening to enough people over a long enough span of time. When some fluky or scary coincidence takes place, when events cluster into a pattern against which the odds seem nearly infinite, the people involved are, of course, overwhelmed with surprise and may start speculating that occult or mystical or psychic forces are at work. "It couldn't have happened just by chance!" they protest. Randomness theory: "Pooh-pooh. Anything can happen by chance." As Martin Gardner puts it, trillions of events, large and trivial, happen to billions of humans every day on earth. In this vast turbulent sea of endless happenings, it would be astonishing if coincidences didn't occur from time to time.

One of Dr. Warren Weaver's favorite coincidences took place many years ago in Beatrice, Nebraska. As *Life* reported the event, 15 people were due to show up at a church for choir practice at 7:20 one wintry evening. In the past there had been a lot of stress on strict punctuality among these 15 men and women. None of them liked the practice sessions to last too late, and it irritated the more punctual members to arrive on time and then wait around for stragglers to drift in. Thus promptness was the rule. But on this particular night all 15 people, including the choirmaster, were late. They were late for at least 10 different reasons. One man couldn't get his car started, and a married couple had trouble finding a babysitter, and so on.

The church, therefore, was still empty shortly before 7:30. That was when the building was destroyed by a disastrous explosion emanating from the furnace. Nobody was there, so nobody was killed.

Some of the choir members and other Beatrice citizens talked, very understandably, of Providence, the protecting hand of God. Some talked of precognition, mysterious hunches, peculiar ghostly impressions: "I had this funny feeling there was a reason for being late. . . ." Others talked of Destiny, the stars, preordained outcomes: "It wasn't their time to die. . . ." And of course everybody talked about luck in one of these forms or another.

Dr. Weaver also talks about luck. To him, however, the Beatrice church incident was nothing more than a lucky coincidence, a coming together of random events in a way that seemed meaningful but had no purposeful or steering force behind it. After all, tardiness is not uncommon. To find 15 people late for an appointed gathering is probably less rare than to find 15 on time. It seems like a safe guess to say that situations of 100 percent tardiness, in which a dozen or so people all turn up somewhere late despite requests for promptness, happen every day. Most of these situations pass unnoticed because there is nothing interesting about them. The Beatrice church episode made news because an explosion occurred, and the explosion made an ordinary and otherwise uninteresting situation seem to take on a numinous meaning.

Dr. Weaver also reports a more trivial but, in its way, more startling coincidence involving a man named Kenneth D. Bryson. Passing through Louisville, Kentucky, on a business trip, Bryson decided on impulse to stop for a day and look around that lively city. He checked in at a hotel recommended by a stranger. To his utter astonishment, he found a letter waiting for him at the hotel. The letter had both his name and room number correct: "Kenneth D. Bryson, Room 307." Ah, sweet mystery! The letter had been mailed before Bryson even knew he would stop over in Louisville, and of course before he knew what hotel he would stay at or what room he would get.

The explanation, as it developed, was as strange as the fact of the letter itself. The previous occupant of the same room in the same hotel had been another man with the same name, Kenneth D. Bryson.

Odd? Certainly, but not in violation of the probability laws. Bryson might have searched for some mystical meaning in this strange episode, but the randomness people would counsel him not to be too impressed. The story merely demonstrates that what can happen, will. If millions of people check in and out of hotels every year, sooner or later two people of the same name will cross paths.

As a mathematician, Martin Gardner is fascinated by numerical coincidences. Some people believe these aren't mere chance patternings. Gardner, being a randomness man (and a more than normally assertive one at that), insists they are. He recalls an incident when a New Jersey suburban commuter train fell into Newark Bay, killing many people. The story was reported widely on TV and in newspapers. One eye-catching news photo showed the train's rear car being pulled from the water, and the car's number was clearly visible: 932.

Among those who noted that number with interest were several thousand policy players in Manhattan. People who play the numbers often attach occult significance to numbers that appear in the news. To them, that 932 so prominently displayed on the front pages was a clear betting signal. Thousands bet on that number that day—and, astoundingly, it turned up as the randomly picked winning number.

Martin Gardner's assessment: the mystical 932

showed up in two places by sheer chance, not because of any occult forces. Such coincidences have happened before and will happen again.

Coincidences happen to everybody. Most of them are trivial and elicit nothing more than a vague feeling of puzzlement, a grin, a shrug. Something reminds you of a long-gone friend whom you haven't thought of for years, and the phone rings and it's your friend. You encounter a word you've never seen before and look it up in a dictionary, and over the next few days the word pops up in everything you read. You've been job-hunting for months and nothing has turned up, and then you suddenly get three offers on the same day. These are common human experiences. They form part of the evidence that is offered in support of some intriguing and hard-to-prove theories about luck, but to randomness disciples they illustrate nothing more than the expected workings of the probability laws.

As the iconoclasts of luck, randomness people are always in the position of hosing down other people's fine poetic fires. A stroke of luck is always surprising and mysterious to the man or woman who experiences it and often give rise to religious or occult or psychical speculation. The randomness theory demands of its disciples that they damp that speculation wherever they find it. I have never met one who actually said "pooh-pooh," but you can always hear that prim little remark somewhere in the background of their words, like the memory of a distant school bell ringing when you were out on the street having fun. This philosophical position unavoidably makes for a certain prickly quality in randomness people, a certain lack of joy and verve. They are always having to say, "It is not as interesting as it seems."

Sometimes this assessment, "not interesting," is mainly subjective. Other people, looking at the same situation from other viewpoints, may find it highly interesting and many think they have good reasons. For example, consider the hard luck that plagued Marie-Thérèse Nadig, a Swiss skier in the 1976 Winter Olympics in Innsbruck, Austria. She was one of the most noted skiers in that stellar gathering, a holder of many awards, seemingly with excellent chances to win medals in both the downhill and the slalom. Because of what seemed like outrageously bad luck, she went home with nothing.

Shortly before she came to Innsbruck, Marie-Thérèse Nadig lost a lucky charm that she had long carried with her, a tiny pair of crossed gold skis. It was only a bauble, hardly valuable except for sentimental and perhaps occult reasons. Some of her friends were concerned over the loss. She said she wasn't.

When she got to Innsbruck, planning to practice daily, she was quickly struck down by hard luck in the form of the flu. She had to spend days in bed.

She struggled out of bed a few days before the downhill race and went out onto the slopes to practice. More hard luck arrived. She slipped and sprained her shoulder so badly that she had to drop out of that race.

There was still the slalom. She started down the hill in what seemed like good form. Then, abruptly, the handle came off one of her poles. With admirable pluck, she tried to finish the race. But it was a tough course even for a skier with both poles. With only one, it was impossible.

Sports enthusiasts, like gamblers and theatrical folk and some other breeds, are notably concerned with the role of luck in success or failure and tend to talk of it in mystical terms. Many at Innsbruck, and many TV watchers in America, felt the forces of destiny had ganged up on the luckless Swiss skier for unknown purposes (perhaps in order to grant good luck to the other women who did win those two races). There was, of course, no evidence whatever that this was so, but the speculation made the Nadig story more appealing, somehow more tidy.

A randomness man I met at a cocktail party, an

American Can engineer, grouchily stamped the story with the official randomness label: "not interesting." He pointed out that flu was epidemic in the Olympic Village at the time, so it was not at all surprising that a certain Swiss skier was among those infected. He speculated that the next piece of bad luck, the sprained shoulder, may well have resulted from general weakness and wobbliness, a residue of the sickness. Thus the flu and the shoulder injury should be considered as one unlucky break, not two. As for the lost ski pole, "Well, things are always breaking and falling apart. What's so amazing about that?"

He couldn't actually prove it was uninteresting. He only felt it was.

In some cases, however, the randomness theory can prove mathematically that a certain story is less amazing than it seems. There are certain kinds of coincidences and apparent strokes of luck and other situations in which our common sense fools us badly. The situations seem wildly unlikely, seem to violate the laws of probability, but in fact the laws are always working perfectly well. The situations are much more likely to happen than we think.

When I was in the army, for instance, the 100-odd men in my outfit were told one day to line up in birthday order, starting with January 1 and ending with December 31. The reason for this exercise eludes my memory, but it produced what I thought was an interesting result. Two other men and I discovered to our surprise that we had all been born on the same date in three consecutive years: June 28 1927, 1928, and 1929. Over the next couple of months we waxed mystical over this, drank a lot of beer together, philosophized about Life and Death and Destiny and other grand things. One of my birthday-mates had a girlfriend who was an astrologer, and she enhanced the awesomeness of it all by divining that we had been brought together by an Unseen Power. As long as our mystic bond wasn't broken, she proclaimed, the Power would guide us into good luck.

Well, maybe. But mature reflection makes plain that the coming together of three birthday-mates under those circumstances was far from surprising—indeed was quite expectable. The consecutive-years business, in the first place, was entirely without mystery. All 100 members of that outfit were young men, none younger than 18, very few older than the early twenties. Nearly all of us had been born between 1926 and 1930.

So much for the years. As for the month and day, June 28, that apparent coincidence was simply a demonstration of something called the "birthday paradox," with which students of probability law like to confound people. There is no need to go into the mathematics of the paradox here, but it turns out that the coming together of people with matched birthdays is much more probable than intuition or common sense would tell us. All you need do is bring 23 people together, and the odds become better than 50-50 that there will be at least one pair of people in group who have the same birthday. With 50 people the odds in favor of that outcome are better than 30 to 1. With 100 people the odds are better than 3 million to 1, which is to say the outcome is nearly certain.

In my outfit of 100-plus men, therefore, it would have been astounding *not* to find at least one pair of birthday-mates. In fact, as it turned out, there were three other pairs in addition to our triple match—which is just about what the laws of probability would predict. Our three-of-a-kind was more rare than a pair, but the odds against it weren't all that high. In a group of 100, there is about one chance in three of finding such a triple match.

Randomness people also cultivate a casual attitude toward runs of luck, which fascinate everybody else. A "run," as usually defined, is a species of coincidence in which bits of good or bad luck get clumped together in a certain time span or sequence of win-lose events. Everybody experiences such runs. There are days when everything you touch turns to gold, and there are other days when everything turns to—well, let us be polite and call it dust and ashes. If you play bridge or poker or some other card game, you are keenly aware that there are nights when you pick up one golden hand after another, and there are other nights when you wish you had gone to the movies instead.

Such runs demand explanation. If we are talking about playing bridge or poker for small stakes or no stakes, runs are unimportant beyond the boundaries of the game itself. If we are talking about high-stakes gambling, or investment, or business decision-making, or the daily feinting and parrying with which we struggle toward personal goals, then the phenomenon of runs becomes massively important because it can influence the entire course of a life. But a run is equally mysterious whether it occurs in a neighborhood bridge game or in some desperate gamble with one's life savings. What causes it?

The randomness theory offers its usual sensible-sounding and faintly surly explanation. Runs of luck? Naturally. When events are happening at random, they are bound to bunch and cluster here and there. No beach is perfectly level. The random effects of wind and waves and tides create hills of sand here, valleys there.

It is even possible to make mathematical predictions about the degree and frequency of such clustering. If you toss a coin enough times, you expect it to land tails up on roughly half the tosses. The more often you toss it, the more closely you are likely to approach that 50-percent-tails expectation predicted by the probability laws. That is the expected long-term result. But the laws of probability don't demand that the tosses alternate with perfect regularity, heads-tails-heads-tails. On the contrary, the laws predict that there will be runs of heads from time to time, and also runs of tails.

44

The Psychic Theories

If you toss a coin 1,024 times, says Professor Weaver, you can expect that there will probably be one run in which tails comes up eight times in a row. This isn't guaranteed to happen. The statistics say only that it is more likely to happen than not. If you bet on its happening, in other words, the odds are that you will win. Similarly, in that same series of 1,024 tosses the odds are with you if you bet that there will be two runs of seven tails in a row, four runs of six in a row, and eight runs of five in a row.

The same laws apply to any other random this-way-that-way or yes-no situation—the glamorous old game of roulette, for instance. There are dozens of different ways to bet on a roulette wheel, but three types of bets are exactly like betting on the toss of a coin. You can bet on red or black, on odd or even numbers, or on low or high numbers (1–18 or 19–36). These are the so-called even-money bets. If you bet a dollar and win, you get another dollar and thus double your money. Some roulette players jump from one kind of bet to another, but the more typical breed of players picks a certain thing to bet on during a given evening—often as the result of a mystic hunch or omen—and doggedly sticks with that same bet. He or she might bet repeatedly on even numbers, for example. If you bet that way, obviously you hope there will be runs of even numbers during the time when you and your money are at the table.

The laws of probability say there should be runs of even, and indeed there are (and runs of odd and red and everything else too). At Monte Carlo once, even came up 28 times in a row. If you had been there that night and had started by betting a dollar on even and had let your money ride, so that it doubled each time, after the twenty-eighth coup or turn of the wheel you would have had a little more than $134 million. House limits on the sizes of bets would have forbidden such a procedure, but it is still pleasant to dream about.

If you had stayed put for the twenty-ninth coup,

45

however, you would have lost everything, including your original dollar. One weeps to think about that, and it illustrates a drawback of the randomness theory. The theory can tell us in general terms what to expect, but it can't tell us when.

Probability law can tell us that a run of 28 even numbers in a row should occur roughly once in every 268 million coups of a roulette wheel. But that piece of knowledge is only of limited help to you when you sit down to bet. You can't know when that run will occur. It is virtually certain to occur again on some wheel somewhere sometime if people keep playing roulette long enough, but nobody knows whether it will happen this year at Las Vegas or a century hence in some casino not yet dreamed of. Moreover, if a run of even numbers gets started and stretches to four, five, six in a row, you have no way of knowing when it will stop. Are you in at the beginning of a run of 28, and should you therefore let your money ride? Or will the run stop at six, and should you take your winnings and quit?

When should you start betting and when should you stop? How long will the run of luck last? Randomness theory has no answers to offer. It admits total helplessness in the face of these questions.

In this sense, luck is an unmanageable element in randomness theory—unmanageable whether in games of chance or in the more serious business of living (which is itself a huge game of chance). The theory can pronounce the odds for and against a given outcome, but there it stops, baffled. When I told Martin Gardner I was going to write a book about luck, he suggested that maybe I shouldn't. He found the topic too "amorphous." In the light of the randomness theory, of course, it is. Luck is just something that happens. There is nothing sensible you can say or do about it.

Professional gamblers, who deal daily in the distilled essence of luck, tend to feel for this reason that there is something missing in the randomness theory. Most of

The Psychic Theories

them feel the element of luck can be managed better than that theory manages it. Luck to them is more tangible, more real: a thing that has a separate existence rather than merely being a label for the outcomes of random events.

One such man is Major A. Riddle, president of the Dunes Club in Las Vegas. A few years ago he wrote a fascinating text, *The Weekend Gambler's Handbook,* and in it he made the following complaint: "Luck . . . is the only element that has rarely been incorporated into gambling theory. Understanding luck is as integral a part of gambling as is knowing how to cut down the odds against you."

His view of luck is clearly different from that of proponents of the randomness theory. He has studied that theory with care, and in the *Handbook* he presents various probability calculations with which no randomness man could find fault. But then he goes further and talks of luck as a separate entity. He sees it as something that can give you additional help (or additional problems) beyond statistical odds.

For instance, he counsels you to "test" your luck before embarking on any venture, whether it is a gambling game or something of greater personal meaning. If you walk into a casino, he says, you should place a few small bets "to see how your luck is running that day." If it turns out to be running nicely, then you place larger bets.

To a randomness proponent, this is sheer nonsense. The mere fact that a run of luck has started, says the randomness theory, is no indication that it will continue. When you place your next bet, the odds for and against you are precisely the same as they always were, whether or not that bet has been preceeded by a run of luck in previous bets. Thus any talk of "testing" luck is inane.

Not to Major Riddle, however, and not to a lot of other gamblers and investment speculators and general

47

chance-takers. Riddle insists that luck is a mysterious force that somehow (he doesn't know how) improves or lowers the odds in a given person's favor over a given span of time. There are people who think they know how, but Riddle modestly offers no theories on this point. He says only that runs of luck, when they come, can be seen coming in advance and within certain limits can be managed.

He tells about a newspaperman who stopped in at the Dunes one evening with $20 in his pocket. He placed a few small side bets at a crap table. He won the bets. To Riddle, who was standing at his side, this was a signal that the newsman's luck was running high that night. In gamblers' parlance, the man was "hot." Accordingly, Riddle counseled larger and larger bets. The newsman stayed hot and went on winning. Thus a run of luck was successfully seized and used. But now there was a new question to be answered: When would the run stop? Should the newsman go on betting even larger amounts and risk losing it all if the run abruptly subsided? Riddle had a feeling the run was beginning to peter out and urged the newsman to quit. The man didn't want to, but his luck was so good that night, as Riddle tells the story, that luck itself solved the problem for him. He had been drinking heavily all evening. He passed out.

When he sobered up and stumbled to breakfast the next morning, Riddle handed him his winnings: $21,265.

Randomness advocates acknowledge that such adventures can happen and might even happen often, but they stolidly doubt that runs of luck can be detected in advance or managed in Riddle's sense. As they would interpret the newsman's story, he won simply because events chanced to cluster into a pattern that was favorable to him. Nothing "caused" this clustering. Nothing made it more likely to happen to him that night than any other night, nor more likely to happen to him than to somebody else.

The very idea of somebody being "hot" in the gamblers' sense is perfect nonsense to any randomness disciple. When you say somebody is hot, you imply that he or she is temporarily more luck-prone than normal. Luck-proneness of this kind simply does not exist in the universe of randomness.

Harry Walden,* chronic gambler and nearly chronic loser. He is 55, has never married, lives alone and says he doesn't mind. He is a small, spare man with a big nose and an engaging grin. At one time or another he has been a bus driver, taxi driver, truck driver, and shoe salesman. At the moment he is unemployed. This is fine by him, for it allows him more time to visit Yonkers, Aquaduct, and other racetracks around New York.

Harry has not had much success in life, and the odd thing is that he doesn't mind saying so. Such a man is rare. He tells his story with great cheer and even a certain wild grace. He is impeccably generous when he has money and doesn't complain when he hasn't. You might say he is a man who is detached from the luck in his life. He watches it come and go with some interest but without great personal involvement. It is reasonable to suppose he cares, but he doesn't seem to care very much. To him, life is so filled with randomness that no meaning or purpose can be discerned in it. Instead of trying to make order out of the randomness or argue with it, he simply shrugs and gives in to it. He throws himself on its mercy by betting whenever he has money to bet.

"You win some, you lose some," he says cheerily. "I done some stupid things in my life. I been in the slammer a couple times, once for stealing money to pay off

* Pseudonym.

a bookie, and I been picked up on drunk and disorderly a few times too. I don't drink anymore, though. Three years ago a doctor tells me, 'Harry,' he says, 'you got two choices. Either you plug a cork in that bottle or you ain't gonna live till next year.' So I quit cold. I got some family members, they ask why I don't quit playing the ponies too. They tell me, 'Harry, you clown, if you could quit drinking, you could quit gambling too.' But see, I don't see a reason to quit gambling. I tell them, 'What the hell,' I says, 'it ain't killing me, is it? I'm still here, right?' Right. Way I see it, everybody got a right to enjoy their own harmless fun. Besides, maybe one day I'll hit big. I sure as hell won't ever get rich any other way."

I ask Harry if this is why he likes the horses: that he sees them as his one great hope of wealth. He laughs. "Hope? No, I wouldn't say hope exactly. It's something that could happen, that's all. If it happens, terrific, but I'd be in the bughouse by now if I sat around and did a lot of hoping. Hope can kill you, you know that? No, I just take it the way it gets served up. Some days you got luck. Like here's a frinstance. I'm out at the track a few weeks ago. I been losing all day. I'm tapped out, I mean really tapped out. I'm not gonna have enough money to buy a can of beans. In the fifth race I'm down to my last two bucks. There's a change of jockeys. It feels lucky to me, so I decide to go with it and bet the long shot, two bucks to win. I win. I'm going to get some bucks. Not a lot, but some. So I'm walking over to collect, and what do I find on the ground? Two ten-dollar win tickets on the same horse. Somebody threw them away by mistake. Now this is *real* bread. I walk out with about eight hunnabucks in my pocket. That night, luck was my lady.

"But now you take some other times. I win pretty big sometimes, but I never win really big, and that's why I'm almost always broke. I got a history of putting my money on the wrong horse in a photo finish. The

50

near miss, that's my life story, and all around me I see other guys winning a bundle and sometimes I even help them do it. It's like luck passes through me and hits the guy standing next to me. Listen, I'll tell you a story. I'm down at Yonkers one night. I have the twin double, right? I have this fifty-to-one shot. Her name is Sugar Hill Millie, I'll never forget that name. I put my money on her, and she comes in. Photo finish. They keep us waiting for ten minutes. Finally it turns out my horse loses. I came *that* close to walking out of there with, like, six grand. That would have been a nice night's work. Instead I go home with zilch.

"But listen, there's more to this story. On my way home I stop for a cup of coffee at this diner where some of us hang out. There's this guy and his wife there. They been at the track all day but they lost a bundle and left early, figured it wasn't their day. The guy looks gloomy as hell, like nothing he does that day is gonna turn out right. He sees me come in and says, "Hey, Harry, you see the twin double? Who came in?' I tell him, 'Don't ask,' I says, 'I'm too depressed. I think it was number seven.' The guy jumps up and says, 'Holy cow, that's my horse!' And he grabs his wife, leaves his English muffin on the table and hustles back to the track. He collects five grand, this guy. He was so sure he was gonna lose, he would have thrown his tickets away if I hadn't happened to come in at just the right time."

Does Harry have any theory about luck? None.

"It doesn't make any sense," he says. "There's no way to figure it. You got one guy, he's upstanding, right? He supports his old grandma, he pays his taxes, he buys poppies from war veterans. Anybody comes knocking at his door for charity, he kicks in a couple of bucks. Then you got another guy, he'd steal the shoes off a baby and sell them. Who wins? The wrong guy just as often as the right guy. Nah, you can't make any sense of it. You ever find out what luck means, you tell me."

Harry looks morose for a second. Then his grin returns. "Ah, the hell with it," he says. "You lose today, you win tomorrow. There's always tomorrow, right?"

2.

The Psychic Theories

DR. ROBERT BRIER looked me straight in the eye and said he had an infallible system for winning at roulette.

Infallible? That's a strong word. I asked Dr. Brier if he really meant it. He said he certainly did. He even added another strong word and called the system *unequivocally* infallible. He and a colleague have tested it again and again in casinos from Las Vegas to Curaçao, he said, and they have never failed to leave with more money than they brought.

This was weird. Martin Gardner had told me, just as unequivocally, "Nobody wins regularly at roulette unless the game is rigged and they're in on the rigging. Naturally the casinos like to keep the myth going because it brings in players." I had studied all kinds of roulette systems invented through the centuries and had convinced myself, with help from Gardner and others, that none could work. Many such systems look plausible and appealing at first glance, and because of that, many have survived for a long time. Some can diminish the risk of a large loss, but they also diminish, by equal proportion, the chance of a large win. None can cut down the house odds against which you must play. Essentially all systems are alike: you win if you are lucky.

Yet here was Dr. Bob Brier telling me a different story. Brier is a professor of philosophy at Long Island University's C. W. Post College. He is a lean, curly-haired, cheerful, energetic man in his early thirties. For most of his life he has been interested in parapsychology—the study of psychic or "psi" phenomena, which are alleged but unproved human powers such as the ability to read others' thoughts (telepathy), to know the future (clairvoyance or precognition), and to move or influence physical objects by direct mental force (psychokinesis). Brier's "infallible" roulette system depends on precognition.

How does it work and what is its rationale?

"Obviously," he says, "if you could read the future infallibly, you could beat a roulette wheel infallibly. If you always knew in advance whether red or black was going to come up, you could sit there happily doubling and redoubling your money every night until you hit the house limit. Now, there *are* people who can foretell the future, but none can do it infallibly, and this has always been a major frustration in parapsychology. A given person might have his or her psi powers working beautifully today but not tomorrow. In guessing cards or roulette outcomes, this person might score 10 percent above chance expectations over a long run of attempts, but during that long run there could be many short periods when the psi wasn't working. You can see the problems that come up when you apply this to gambling. If you got this person to help you play roulette nonstop for a whole month, you'd come out ahead in the end. But that approach wouldn't be practical. You'd need a big cash reserve to keep you in the game on days when the psi failed. What's more, you'd be bored to death."

This difficulty was the major problem that Dr. Brier

tackled in constructing his infallible system. Essentially, this is what he did:

He sought the help of a woman student, whom he identifies only as H.B. She had previously demonstrated strong precognitive talent to his and other's satisfaction. He got her to make predictions—red or black —on 50 spins or coups of a roulette wheel in a specified casino at a specified date and hour in the future. She repeated this process a number of times over a span of days, so that there were a lot of predictions on each of the 50 spins. Brier then recorded the majority vote of all the predictions on each coup. In predicting the first coup, for instance, she foresaw black more often than red, so he recorded the prediction as black. In this way, he hoped, the problem of unreliability would be diminished.

Then on the specified date, he went to the specified casino at Curaçao with his friend Walter Tyminski. Tyminski is a devoted gambler and president of Rouge et Noir, Inc., a company that publishes gambling texts and newsletters. With H.B.'s averaged predictions in hand, Brier and Tyminski watched the roulette wheel without betting for a number of spins. H.B.'s predictions turned out to show a seemingly reliable deviation from plain chance expectation. Thereupon the two happy gamblers began to bet on the remainder of the 50 coups, guided, of course, by the remainder of the predictions. They bet lightly at first, then more heavily. They left considerably richer than they had arrived. Brier declines to say how much richer.

If psi powers did exist, they would be very helpful in explaining luck. But the study of psychic phenomena is a strange business. Its devotees want it to be classed as a science (and I have so classed it here), but the other sciences have not wished to accord it full membership in their club. To date, the best that can be said is that it has won a kind of provisional second-class membership.

Speculations: Scientific

Some physicists, biologists, and other scientists think psychic phenomena do exist and parapsychology is a worthwhile field of study. Others think it might be worthwhile but tend to doubt it. Still others think it is a form of occultism dressed up in academic clothing. And finally, some think it is plain, old-fashioned hogwash.

The problem is that it deals with forces that can't be measured or satisfactorily described—at any rate, haven't been yet. Worse, even if you grant that the postulated forces might exist, it is very hard to imagine how they would work. If H.B. can sit in New York and foresee what a roulette wheel will do in Las Vegas or Curaçao next month, how does that information find its way into her head? With what form of energy, transmitted in what way, through what channels? Parapsychologists keep trying to invent answers, but they only succeed in making the very question sound sillier.

As Dr. Brier mournfully noted in the journal *Social Policy,* "Parapsychology is the science that studies phenomena which cannot be explained from within the conceptual schema of modern physics." If psi phenomena do exist, there is nothing in modern science to explain them, at least science as we know it here in the West. Some Eastern sciences and philosophies appear to make more room for the possibility of psi forces. But to the Western scientist, with his insistence that experiments be repeatable and his powerful yearning for a sensible theory to explain whatever effects are observed, psychic phenomena are a baffling puzzle—and, if he grants or suspects their existence, a damned nuisance. He would be happier if they would go away and stop bothering him.

It seems unlikely that they will. On the other hand, it also seems unlikely that they will win complete acceptance in the scientific community or the world at large, at least in our lifetimes. The safest prediction is that the debate about them will continue. Parapsychologists will keep producing evidence to show that the alleged phenomena exist, and other scientists will keep shooting the evidence down.

Much of the evidence produced to date has come from laboratory tests in which people guessed what cards were being turned up beyond their range of hearing or vision. Dr. Joseph Banks Rhine, a young botanist, popularized this card-guessing approach in the 1920s and more or less invented the science of parapsychology. (Before that, the study of these phenomena had been decidedly in the "occult" category.) Rhine and his disciples kept coming up with human showpieces: people who displayed an apparently uncanny ability to "know" what they couldn't know through the five ordinary senses.

Each parapsychologist had his own favorite showpiece. Rhine's for a long time was Hubert Pearce, a divinity student. Rhine and Pierce played with special test cards, 25 to a deck, each card marked with one of five symbols. If you had no talent for extrasensory perception and made random guesses about the order in which the cards would turn up, the statistical probability would be that you would score 5 correct in each run of 25. Pearce, for a time, averaged closer to 10 hits per run and once even scored a perfect 25. The chance of getting that perfect score through random coincidence is microscopic. "It could not have happened by sheer chance," Rhine insisted. "Therefore some other force must be at work, and therefore we are required to accept the existence of ESP."

Other parapsychologists turned up with still more amazing showpieces. According to the *Guiness Book of World Records,* the most amazing of all was produced in 1936 by Professor Bernard Reiss of Hunter College, New York. His prize exhibit was a 26-year-old woman. In a series of 74 runs through one of those 25-card decks, Reiss claimed, she had one perfect score of 25, two of 24, and an overall average of 18.24. The odds against her getting that average score by chance, says

Speculations: Scientific

Guiness, are represented by a 10 followed by 700 zeros. Professor Reiss, of course, echoed Dr. Rhine: "It couldn't have happened by chance, so . . ."

So nothing, said a chorus of other scientists. Dr. Warren Weaver, the randomness man, is among those who are not impressed. He would remind us of the first two probability laws: that anything can, and hence will, happen. The high scores of Hubert Pearce and others, says Dr. Weaver, can be viewed simply as unusual runs of random luck. Dr. Weaver admits that the odds against such runs are enormous and that the runs therefore seem "strange," hard to believe in terms of plain randomness. But he insists that the randomness interpretation is no harder to believe than Dr. Rhine's. Rhine had to choose between two "strange" interpretations, and he arbitrarily chose the one that *he* felt was the more likely. Dr. Weaver believes Rhine chose the wrong one. "I cannot accept his interpretation."

It would be convenient if Dr. Rhine were right, however. If it is ever proved conclusively that ESP exists, that will go a long way toward explaining why some people are luckier than others. The luckiest men and women, in this conceptual scheme, would be those with the strongest psychic abilities.

If you could read other people's minds, even part of the time and even indistinctly, that would greatly improve your luck in poker, business, love, and shopping for a used car. If you could know parts of the future, even imprecisely, that would make you a winner at Las Vegas and in the stock market. In a thousand endeavors from finding a job to buying a lottery ticket, it would put you in the right places at the right times. If you could influence physical objects with direct mental power, even clumsily, that would also be of inestimable value. You could control the roll of dice or the shuffling of cards—perhaps not all the time and perhaps inexactly, but enough to turn the odds to your favor. You could will your lottery ticket to rise to the top of a barrel and get picked. You could deflect a car that would otherwise have run you over. You could . . .

Oh, well. Such notions make lovely daydreams, but we had better not let them dull the cutting edge of skepticism. As many scientists have sourly pointed out, a salient feature of all psi research is that there are so many of these very nice dreams behind it. It deals with powers that every human being would wish to have. These wishes undoubtedly churn and bubble inside parapsychologists as in everybody else.

Still, a lot of evidence points to the possibility that Rhine chose the right alternative. People like Dr. Rhine and Dr. Brier are not fools, after all. If they tell us something exists, we had better listen with care before trying to reach conclusions of our own. Let's hear what their research has turned up.

Fashions in psychic research seem to come and go. The three basic theories—on the existence of telepathy, precognition, and telekinesis—rise and fall in relative popularity as the decades roll on. Many researchers buy all three, but others favor only one or two. Some, for example, find the idea of telepathy easier to swallow than the other two, for it seems easier to imagine how telepathy might work. If H.B. can read my mind, that is weird but not as weird as the idea that she can see into the future. Telepathy doesn't seem to violate known physical laws so badly. My mind is here, after all, a lump of busy stuff that (to me) plainly exists. I feel its relays and synapses buzzing and clicking. It is presumably generating some kind of energy, and conceivably some leakage or echo of that energy could reach H.B.'s mind. Thus the notion of mind-to-mind communication has dominated psi research in some periods, and in fact it was the notion with which Rhine and Pearce began their historic card games.

Today, however, the field is dominated by studies of precognition. This has been the fashion since the early 1960s or thereabouts. Noted clairvoyants like Jeane Dixon, who claims to have foreseen great strokes of national bad luck such as both Kennedys' assassinations, have captured not only the public's imagination but also that of the psi research community. To make this chapter fashionable as well as reasonably brief, let's confine ourselves mainly to studies of precognition. Whatever is said about precognition will apply fairly accurately to the other two psychic theories as well.

There are many groups in America and the world that are studying precognition and other psi phenomena today. Oddly, some of the most prominent (and in many ways the most weird) are in the world's most stubbornly materialistic country, Soviet Russia. Probably the most prominent and respected in the United States is ASPR, the American Society for Psychical Research. Its publications list many renowned thinkers as present and past members, including Sigmund Freud. It inhabits a dark, hushed, appropriately ghostly old brownstone building near Central Park in New York City. The research director is Dr. Karlis Osis, a tall, thin man who was born in Latvia and speaks in scholarly, heavily accented English.

Dr. Osis is interested in all aspects of psi research, but particularly in precognition. "I am intrigued by lottery winners," he told me. "There has been some research on this recently, and it appears that precognition may play a role in many cases. The person is walking along the street, not thinking of lotteries at all, and then comes a sudden hunch: 'I must go into this store and buy a lottery ticket. The ticket will win.' The person buys the ticket, and it does win. This seems to be a quite common occurrence."

It is, and there are many strange stories to tell. Twenty-three-year-old Robert Bronson felt sure he would win a special Christmas lottery in Maryland a few years ago. He bought some tickets, although he had a wife and child and barely enough income to make ends meet. His wife was angry when he came home with his tickets, but—as he later told reporters—he felt curiously calm. One ticket bore repetitions of 7, which he considers his lucky number. He felt unaccountably certain this ticket would win. It began by winning him $500 and qualifying him to enter a final drawing, which was held in a Baltimore auditorium.

Just before the winner's name was to be announced, Bronson stood up. It was as though he had heard his name spoken. People stared at him in the silence. Then the name was spoken, and it was Bronson's. The prize was $1 million.

Dr. Osis is delighted by stories like these. He is even more drawn to stories of multiple lottery winners, men and women who hit the jackpot more often than seems fair. "Such people may have a strong precognitive talent," he says. "Whether they use it consciously or not, it may be the basic reason for what everybody else calls their good luck."

The conclusion is indeed tempting. If you win once, you figure it's just Dr. Weaver's kind of luck. But if you win more than once, much more often than other people, you must ask why you are so favored. Consider Randy Portner, for instance. He lives in Rome, New York. He is 21 years old. He began playing the state lottery when he was 18. To date he has won prizes 19 times.

Many of the prizes were relatively small: $25, $100. But one was $50,000 and others were more than mere pocket money, and Randy Portner today is comfortably wealthy for a man so young. He might be wealthier, but the New York State lottery was suspended for a long time pending investigations of alleged mismanagement.

"I can't explain why I win so often," he told me. "I bought tickets fairly regular, but no more than a lot of other people I know who never won a dime. I started when I got out of high school and went to work in a grocery store. They sold tickets in the store, and I'd buy them in weeks when I had some spare cash and felt lucky. It's funny, this thing about feeling lucky.

Some weeks I had a feeling it wouldn't do any good to buy tickets. I was sure I'd lose, almost like I knew there were no winning tickets in the store. Other weeks I'd have this feeling there was a winning ticket in there somewhere, so I'd pick out a few and buy them, and a lot of the time I'd win at least something. It was crazy. Like I said, I can't really explain it. Other guys would buy losers all the time and come around and ask me, 'Why don't I ever win?' What could I tell them? I didn't know why."

Randy Portner seems dubious about his precognitive talent, if he has one. Dr. Osis, puzzling over this and similar cases, is less dubious. "How else," he asks, "can you explain why some people never win anything—never, *never*—while others win a dozen times or more? I cannot believe it is just chance."

Dr. Osis is also interested in the role of precognition in avoiding accidents. Much interesting material has been written on this topic, as well as a good deal of nonsense. It all seems to have started with the sinking of the ocean liner *Titanic* in 1912. More than 1,500 lives were lost. For months afterward, newspaper and magazine editors filled space with stories of people who might have been aboard but for some reason weren't. The standard headline went: "A (Blank) Saved me." Fill in the blank with your choice of the following words and phrases: Dream; Hunch; Lucky Accident; Fortune Teller; Vision in Church; Child's Plea; Dog. Ever since then, major disasters have been a signal to editors that a new sheaf of such stories should be dug up—or, if necessary, invented. The trouble with these stories is that they are all told after, rather than before, the disaster that was allegedly foreseen or sidestepped, and few such tales are adequately documented.

One avid collector of disaster-prediction accounts for many years was Dr. Louisa Rhine, wife of the parapsychologist. She was convinced that at least some people, at least sometimes, have the ability to sense bad luck coming their way and so are able to sidestep it. In *Hid-*

den Channels of the Mind she told of a mother who awoke one night from a strange dream. The mother lived in a rickety old house, and in the dream she saw the house being shaken by a violent storm. The shaking loosened an old, heavy chandelier, and it fell onto her baby, who was sleeping in a crib below it.

It was not stormy outdoors when the mother awoke from this frightening dream. In fact the night was clear and calm. Nonetheless, she went to her baby and moved his crib out from under the chandelier.

Stories like this are never quite satisfying because the very telling of the beginning indicates what the end will be. Later that night, it need hardly be said, a sudden storm arose, the old house shook, and the chandelier fell.

Dr. Rhine presumably checked her sources with proper care and convinced herself that the mother's story, though lacking documentation or any possibility of being documented, was true. Still, such tales always leave you wondering: Aren't other explanations conceivable and plausible? Does the story really prove that a precognitive dream occurred? Maybe the chandelier did fall in the manner described, and maybe the mother did indeed move the crib just in time to avoid an unlucky outcome. But perhaps she moved it for some reason other than a foreboding dream. Later, when she saw the heavy chandelier on the floor and imagined what might have been, the stark horror of it tipped her into an emotional state in which she couldn't distinguish past from present, fact from fantasy. The dream may never have occurred, except afterward, while she was awake.

Maybe one problem is that most of us *want* this kind of story to be true. We want it so badly that we sometimes grow too uncritical. I want the mother's story to be true for at least two reasons. In the first place, though the story isn't perfectly satisfying, it is still a tidy tale with a nice little shiver attached. In the second place it leads me to hope that I, too, may have unknown precognitive talents and may sometimes unconsciously use them. The story allows me to speculate that my grip on good luck may be tighter than I know.

Dr. Osis, though he has no trouble accepting such stories as true, does acknowledge that the problem of documentation is a bad one. It is nearly impossible to solve. Dr. Osis knows of one parapsychologist who tried to solve it with what seemed like a clever approach. It was a coldly statistical approach that might have produced quite credible evidence—if only it had worked.

The parapsychologist reasoned thus: "If, as we suppose, there are many people with conscious or unconscious psi, then there should be many who avoid getting on any airplane that is going to crash. Can this be demonstrated and quantified? Quite possibly. All I need do is go to airlines and ask to see their records of seat cancellations and no-shows. If a plane is about to crash, there should be a number of seat holders who fail to get aboard. That number should be greater, on average, than in the case of a comparable plane that isn't about to crash."

Brilliant! Unfortunately the man's research was never conducted. The airlines he approached all felt the study would be bad for their public image.

Margaret Mudrie, housewife. She is 51, friendly, talkative. She comes from Surrey, British Columbia, and she speaks with the clear but (to American ears) oddly accented, vaguely foreign-sounding rhythms of the Canadian west. She considers herself lucky on the whole, but feels her luck is periodic rather than constant. "It comes and goes," she says. "Once in a while I get a sort of flash. I can't quite describe it, but—well, it's a quick sort of feeling that tells me to do something or go somewhere. Like a sudden impulse. It doesn't happen often, but when it comes I know what to do. This has been with me a long time, off and on. It's helped me be mostly lucky. We have a good life, my family and me."

Her husband is an excavator—"he digs holes, big ones, little ones, anything you want"—and they have seven children, of whom four are married. The youngest are still living at home but are self-sufficient, and Margaret Mudrie and her husband occasionally leave for a week's vacation. In winter they are drawn to Nevada, partly for the warm climate and partly for the gambling. "I love playing the slot machines," she says. "I've been told the odds are bad, but I like playing anyway. For me it's recreation."

She is right. The odds are bad. In fact the odds against the player are higher in the standard slots than almost anywhere else in Nevada's garden of risky delights. No randomness devotee who has studied the probability engineering of those noisy and inelegant machines would go anywhere near them. Margaret Mudrie, however, is not a randomness devotee.

On January 22, 1976, the second day of their winter's vacation, she and her husband came to Reno and walked into Harolds Club, known far and wide for its insistence on spelling itself without an apostrophe. Rows and rows of slot machines faced her. "Not many were being used, so I could have picked almost any one. But I walked straight up to one machine that seemed to—I don't know. seemed to be drawing me. It was eerie I had no hesitation about it. I *knew* it was the machine I should play."

It was a machine that ate silver dollars. Margaret Mudrie fed it nine of them and remembers being somewhat puzzled when it simply digested them without even saying thanks. But with her tenth dollar she hit the jackpot that made history.

The machine was of a type called "two-meter progressive." Inside this wonderful invention are two meters or counters that move independently of each other. Each meter displays a number expressing the size of a potential jackpot. Every time somebody drops a coin in the slot and pulls the operating lever, one meter or the other counts upward and increases its number. When you hit the jackpot you randomly hit one meter and get the amount to which it has counted at the time. That meter then returns to its original setting, commonly $5,000 in dollar machines, while the other meter keeps placidly counting upward as though nothing had happened. In such a machine, one meter may be hit several times over the years before the other is hit. Obviously the player's golden hope is to hit a meter that has been counting upward undisturbed for a long, long time.

That is what Margaret Mudrie did. Nobody had touched her meter in years. Her jackpot was the biggest ever paid by a dollar machine in all the long history of Harolds Club. She went home to Canada with $113,232.

3.

The Synchronicity Theory

WE HAVE NOTED before that coincidences prove everything and nothing. We may find it enlightening, however, to look at two more of them at this point. Having looked at them, we will analyze them in the light of a third science-oriented theory about the workings of luck.

This third theory has been given various labels by various of its proponents. Some have called it "synchronicity," some "seriality," some "the clustering effect." To avoid confusion let's settle on e: synchronicity.

Synchronicity has gained less scientific respect (to put it kindly) than either the randomness theory or the psychic theories. As a matter of fact most randomness people would argue that the synchronicity theory doesn't belong in this triad of "scientific" attempts to explain luck. They would urge that it be shifted to the category of "occult" or "mystical" attempts.

To them, this would be a demotion. To believers in the mystical or occult, it would be a promotion. To me, it would be neither. It would be only a change in categories, accompanied by neither dunce cap nor medal. I have chosen to include synchronicity in the "scientific" triad because, despite its occasional mystical overtones, it basically has a Western-pragmatic, science-y sound. Its disciples explain it, or do their best to explain it, more in terms of physics and mathematics and other respected sciences than in terms of the mystical.

Let's see what we can make of it.

The first coincidence story I want to tell you was related to me by Clarence Kelley, director of the FBI. It is an eerie one. It is well known to many of the men and women who work at FBI headquarters in Washington, particularly those who work in the identification section where some 160 million fingerprints are on file. They tell the story to visitors who ask why the FBI puts so much time and effort into those little ink-rolled signatures of fingers and thumbs.

I had put this question to Kelley in the course of a rambling talk about the FBI and its hopes and fears. Kelly is a big genial man in his middle sixties with a pleasant, square, jowly face. When I asked about fingerprints he grinned the grin of a man who loves a good story, leaned back in his chair, lit a cigarette, and said, "Did you ever hear of Will West?"

"No."

Kelly was obviously delighted that I had never heard of Will West, and he proceeded to tell the story. Criminal investigation began to become a science, he said, early in the nineteenth century. One problem that police and forensic scientists wrestled with throughout the century was that of positive identification. If you are investigating a crime and you find a witness who says a certain Joe Smith was on the scene at the time, how can you know for sure if the witness is correct? If a police officer comes forward and says, "Yeah, I know this Smith, he's a hardened criminal, I've arrested him before," and if Smith denies that he even knows what the inside of a police station looks like, how do you find the truth?

What those nineteenth-century criminologists wanted was a coincidence-proof identification method. It is not good enough to say, "I recognize his face," for too many faces look alike. It isn't even unknown in police experience to find oneself dealing with two men or women who not only look alike and dress alike, but whose voices sound alike, who have the same initials, and who are similar in so many coincidental ways that even the sharpest witness is fooled. And so the criminologists wondered: Is there any trait or set of traits that is unique to each human being? Something so unlikely to be duplicated that the element of coincidence can be effectively ruled out?

A French anthropologist, Alphonse Bertillon, offered an answer around 1870. The Bertillon System, as it came to be called, depended on measuring the dimensions of the skull and certain other bony parts of the body. Thousands of measurements by Bertillon himself, and hundreds of thousands more by police agencies in the last three decades of the century, seemed to indicate that this was the long-sought set of unique traits. No two people's Bertillon measurements, not even those of twin brothers or sisters when measured precisely enough, were the same. Furthermore, Bertillon demonstrated that a given man's or woman's measurements could be reduced to a formula that remained unchanged once he or she reached adult size.

Will West entered the story in 1903. His adventure marked the death of the Bertillon System and led to general acceptance of modern identification by fingerprint.

West, convicted of a felony, was sent to the federal penitentiary at Leavenworth, Kansas. Asked about his previous criminal record, he denied having one. He knew that two-time losers were treated less gently and were less likely to win early parole than first offenders, and he staunchly maintained that he had been a law-abiding citizen all his life until now. However, the records officer who admitted him to the penitentiary thought West's face looked familiar. Accordingly, the officer got out his calipers and took West's Bertillon measurements. The officer then went to a file that was cross-indexed according to the Bertillon System and looked for a set of measurements that corresponded to West's. He triumphantly found one. He pulled out the appropriate file card. The name on the card was William West.

"Never served time before, huh?" said the officer. "This card says you're a liar. You not only served time, but you served it right here at Leavenworth."

"I've never seen the place before in my life!" West protested.

"If I believe that," said the officer, "I'd have to believe there are two guys who not only have the same Bertillon measurements but the same name. It couldn't happen in a billion years."

"It just happened!' West yelled.

It had, indeed, just happened. When people finally started listening to Wests protests and did some more checking, they found a cluster of coincidences so startling that it could barely be believed. The second West had been at Leavenworth for a long time and was still there, half forgotten, serving a life sentence for murder. When the two Wests were brought together, their facial and bodily resemblance turned out to be astoundingly close—fully as close as that of twin brothers. If you look at pictures of their two faces today, both in profile and in frontal view, you absolutely cannot tell them apart.

Somebody at Leavenworth was promoting the new idea of fingerprinting at the time, and he saw this curious case as a golden opportunity. He had the two men's prints taken. The two sets of prints bore no resemblance.

Thus did fingerprinting become the preferred method of criminal identification. So far, it has proved the most coincidence-proof of all. Notice that phrase "so far." It isn't actually guaranteed to be coincidence-proof. There is no theoretical reason why it has to be. Next year or a hundred years from now, two people could turn up with identical fingerprints. (Indeed, the first two laws of probability would predict that this will happen eventually.) But as far as the FBI knows, no such case has yet turned up anywhere in the world.

For another odd story, let's turn back to the gambling casinos and to the consideration of our old puzzle, the special type of coincidence called a run of luck. And let's go back even farther in history than the case of Will West. This is the story of the Man Who Broke the Bank at Monte Carlo.

There was a popular song of that name in the Gay Nineties, and it was still being sung occasionally in the 1920s and 1930s. By that time, most hearers assumed it was just a song, probably from some old musical revue or vaudeville act. In fact, however, the song was more in the nature of a musical news report than a fiction. There actually was a man who broke the bank at Monte Carlo, and he did it not once but three times.

I should begin the tale by telling you that this "breaking the bank" business was somewhat less dramatic, financially, than it sounds. It was largely a publicity stunt, originated by a casino manager who wanted to lure new players to his tables. To "break the bank" meant to win all the house money allotted to any one table—an amount which, at the time our story took place, was usually in the neighborhood of 100,-000 French francs. When a player did break a bank, that one table would be closed for the rest of the night and ceremoniously draped in black cloth. The next day, of course, it would be open for business again. The canny manager foresaw correctly that players would flock to that table, believing it to be the focus of a run of bad luck for the house.

Charles Wells, a short, fat, rather mysterious Englishman with an obscure background as a freelance inventor and speculator, turned up at Monte Carlo in 1891 with a couple of hundred francs in his pocket. He went to a roulette table and began betting on *rouge et noir*—red and black, one of the even-money games. He would bet black a few times, then switch to red, then withdraw from betting for a few coups, then plunge back in. He was hot. He won nearly every bet. As the croupier watched at first with interest and then with amazement, he went on winning all night.

He had no apparent "system." Unlike many other roulette players, he carried no little black notebook in which he jotted rows of numbers. He seemed to have no formula by which to guide his play. He was simply, uncannily right. It was almost as though he knew when there would be a run of black, when a run of red, when each would stop. Other players gathered around, furiously scribbling in their notebooks, trying to figure out what his secret system was. But no attempts to elucidate it, nor any attempts to win by making the same bets in the same order, have ever succeeded.

The casino at Monte Carlo, like all casinos everywhere, imposed limits on the size of bets that it would accept. By doubling his money with each win and leaving it in play, Wells quickly reached the limit. That slowed him down, but not enough. Before the night was over, he had broken the bank.

Two nights later he came back and walked to the same table. This time he eschewed the even-money games. He bet in groups of numbers instead. In such games, of which dozens are possible and allowed, the odds against the player on any given coup are greater than in the red-black, odd-even, or *manque-passe* games. But if he wins, his payoff is, of course, proportionately greater. As a hushed and startled crowd watched, Wells proceeded to break the bank a second time.

A few months later, the mysterious Wells turned up

again. This time he played the longest shot of all: betting on single numbers.

The old Monte Carlo roulette wheel bore the numbers from 1 to 36 plus a "house number," 0. (The modern American wheel has two house numbers, 0 and 00.) Thus, if you placed money on any single number at Monte Carlo, your chance of winning on each coup was one in 37. If you did win, you got your bet back plus 35 times that amount. It is a high-risk, high-payoff game, one for people who have nerves of steel, or have a lot of unwanted money to lose, or are drunk.

Wells put money on 5 and left it there. The number 5 came up five times in a row.

The bank was broken again. The mysterious Wells put about 98,000 francs in his pocket and vanished. He never turned up at Monte Carlo again. It is sad and anticlimactic to report that he spent all that money rashly on dubious speculative ventures, got himself tangled in some intractable legal difficulties, and died broke in prison. But at least, in the midst of the miseries that beset him later, he had one stunning and glorious streak of luck to remember.

There are many ways to explain these two peculiar tales—or, to put it less generously and perhaps more precisely, to approach an explanation of them. The randomness theory would say they simply happened and were bound to happen to somebody sooner or later and are therefore less interesting than they seem. Occult theories would talk about guiding stars, lucky numbers. The psychic theories would have no comment to make on the Will West story but would explain the Monte Carlo adventure in terms of either precognition or psychokinesis. This latter theory is espoused, though with a niggle of doubt, by Dr. Bob Brier. He points out that the phenomenon of a given roulette number coming up five times in a row is highly unusual. It can happen by chance, but Brier finds it slightly easier to believe Charlie Wells made it happen. Brier postulates that Wells's "hot" state on all three of his bank-breaking forays was actually a state of abnormally heightened, but temporary, psychic energy.

The synchronicity theory offers an entirely different explanation. This theory holds that adventures like Will West's and Charles Wells's are caused by a mysterious, little understood, but perfectly natural property of the physical universe. This property is a force that somehow brings like together with like. It makes similar or related things cluster in space or time or both. It synchronizes events, creates orderly patterns. It *causes* coincidences.

In other words, says the theory, there is a flaw in the laws of ordinary randomness as they are now understood. If two people look alike and have the same name, like Will and William West, they are more likely to drift together than Martin Gardner's type of probability would predict. And as for runs of luck like Charles Wells's, the synchronicity theory holds that they are more reliable and in a way more predictable than randomness advocates would suppose.

The randomness theory says, of course, that chance events in the past have no effect on chance events in the future. It quarrels with Major Riddle's notion that, once a run of luck has started, you should bet heavily because the run will probably continue. It argues that there is no logical reason why this should be so. The synchronicity theory, by contrast, would grant some merit to Major Riddle's idea. When you experience a run of luck, the synchronists would say, it may be because events of a certain type are being made to cluster together. There is a cosmic *push* toward creation of orderly patterns, and this push (says the theory) was at least partly responsible for Wells's bank-breaking adventure, including his run of five 5's in a row.

The synchronicity idea is the most frustrating of all luck theories because it is so hard to see how, or through what medium, the postulated clustering force would operate. Many synchronists don't even try to explain how. They simply renege. "We can observe that these things happen," they say, "but the nature of the force is beyond human understanding at this stage of scientific development." There is much about the universe that we don't understand, they point out. There are black holes in which space is turned inside out, and subatomic particles that appear to travel backward in time, and many other phenomena that are nightmarishly alien to our daily experiences. The clustering or synchronizing force is another of those phenomena that may be elucidated some day but until then must remain mysterious—not explained, merely noted and humbly acknowledged.

One of the first to suggest the theory and then duck from trying to explain it was a French mathematician of the late seventeenth and early eighteenth centuries, Pierre-Rémond de Montmort. Montmort is less well known today than some of his countrymen and fellow mathematicians, men like Pierre de Fermat and Blaise Pascal, and he is much more obscure than his contemporary and friend, Isaac Newton. Montmort picked up probability calculus where Fermat and Pascal had left it and carried it a great leap forward. Unluckily he died at age 41, and just as unluckily many of his papers and notebooks vanished in the dust and turmoil of the French Revolution.

One modern mathematician who has tried to brighten Montmort's dim reputation is Dr. Florence David, a London University professor. In a delightful historical survey of probability theories, *Games, Gods and Gambling,* she devotes a fair amount of space to his ideas and his strange, short life. Oddly, she seems unimpressed by what may have been a set of profoundly influential elements in shaping those ideas: the conflicts and relationships between practical mathematics and religious mysticism. Montmort was a genuinely pious man who served for a time as a canon at Notre Dame, and he kept seeing what he felt were nonearthly influences in his beloved mathematics. He was especially puzzled and intrigued by coincidences and abnormally long runs of luck—situations in which events didn't happen as randomly as expected and hence were beyond explanation by the mathematics of ordinary probability. He finally gave up and wrote:

"To speak exactly, nothing depends on chance. When one studies nature one is soon convinced that its Creator moves in a smooth, uniform way which bears the stamp of infinite wisdom and prescience. Thus to attach to the word 'Chance' a meaning which conforms with true philosophy, one must think all things are regulated according to certain laws, those which we think depend on chance being those for which the natural cause *is hidden from us*. Only after such a definition can one say that the life of man is a game where chance reigns."

At the time of his too-early death, Montmort was just beginning to toy with the notion that subtle flaws might exist in the laws of probability as worked out by mathematicians. The laws work well on paper but less well when applied to the daily lives of men and women. The laws seem logical, but in that fact may lie the most profound error of all. For our concept of "logic" may itself contain basic flaws. "Logic" is a human construct, after all—a set of laws that seem to work tolerably well for our purposes on earth but may in fact have little to do with the way the rest of the universe works. As mathematician Kurt Goedel has pointed out, we may never discover what those logical flaws are. If our basic system of logic is wrong, it seems unlikely that we will ever identify the wrongness by applying more of the same wrong logic. Thus we may be trapped for all eternity in flawed ways of seeing and thinking, including flawed ways of thinking about luck.

An Austrian biologist, Paul Kammerer, seems to have been the first to give a name to this notion of a different kind of probability. He called it "seriality."

Kammerer, who published most of his thoughts on the subject in the first quarter of this century, was not merely interested in coincidences, he was obsessed by them. He kept a log book in which he recorded instances of seriality that happened to him from about age 20 to age 40. For example, one morning he happened to become curious about a certain rather rare species of butterfly and looked it up in a textbook. That same afternoon he walked past a bookstore, and one book prominently displayed in the window bore a picture of the same butterfly on its cover. That same evening Kammerer saw the butterfly again, this time in person, in a field.

To Kammerer such coincidences were significant. They pointed to some unknown force that, in his view, made like and like come together, made things happen in bunches rather than randomly. Not many other scientists were willing to accord Kammerer the hearing he thought he deserved. Most dismissed him as an eccentric, and some even suspected his log of serial coincidences was partly fiction. There is no evidence that this was so, but the fact that he shot himself dead in 1926, apparently in despair over a scandal involving allegations of faked scientific evidence, is not encouraging.

Carl Jung, the Swiss psychologist-philosopher-mystic, coined the term "synchronicity." His ideas on the topic were much like Kammerer's. He is known today almost entirely for his contributions to psychotherapy, but the fact is he considered his synchronicity theory an important part of his life's work. He, too, collected coincidences. One of his favorites (he is said to have bored friends by incessantly buttonholing people and retelling the story) had to do with a scarab. A woman patient was in his study one day, telling him about a dream whose emotional residue she found troublesome. The dream involved an ornamental scarab, a piece of jewelry fashioned after the colorful African beetle that the ancient Egyptians held sacred. At that moment

Jung heard a tapping on his window. He looked, and there was a large scarabeid beetle, the nearest European equivalent of the scarab.

Aha! said Jung. Synchronicity! There is an unknown "ordering" principle at work in human affairs, he postulated. It is "acausal"—that is, it operates by some mechanism that does not depend on cause and effect as we understand them. The woman patient's dream narrative didn't cause the beetle to bump into Jung's window. Nor did the beetle's random wanderings cause the woman to think about her dream (or cause her to have the dream the night before). Both events were brought together by some force that transcends causality.

Jung did a lot of thinking about this and eventually came up with a theory as to what this "acausal principle" might be. He even prevailed on Wolfgang Pauli, the physicist, to help him write a book about it. Pauli was fully prepared to admit that there are ordering principles in the universe beyond those we can see, and like all physicists then and since, he readily acknowledged that some of these principles might seem outrageously unlikely in terms of ordinary human "logic." But he doesn't seem to have bought Jung's ideas about the nature of the synchronizing or coincidence-making principle. Those ideas are a peculiar blend of psychology, science-fictionish physics, and far-out mysticism. Most of those, including myself, who have tried to understand just what Jung was driving at, haven't.

The man who has probably tried hardest is Arthur Koestler. Koestler is an interesting fellow. He was born in Budapest in 1905, and the first third of his life was marked by wild chance-taking. He worked as a political journalist, drifted around Europe, joined and then quit the Communist Party, landed in a French prison camp in World War II, was released, fought with the British Army. Next he became a novelist, turning out *Darkness at Noon* and other well-regarded books in his adopted tongue, English. The novel-writing phase ended, and since about 1970 he has turned his bright imagination to psychic research and to the theory of synchronicity.

Koestler has become perhaps the leading modern disciple of synchronicity—and without doubt its leading publicity agent. In *The Roots of Coincidence* and later *The Challenge of Chance* (written with two British scientists, Sir Alister Hardy and Robert Harvie), he explains why the synchronicity idea appeals to him and has appealed to others, including Jung. In this he succeeds. He makes the idea highly tempting to anybody who is seeking to explain runs and other puzzling phenomena of luck. But he succeeds less well in his other great effort: to prove that synchronicity belongs in the category of "science." He talks a lot about quantum theory and atomic physics. In his typewriter these are good fun, but their connection with synchronicity is vague at best. Koestler seems to hope the respectability of quantum physics will rub off on synchronicity if he talks about them on the same page.

Still, Koestler's case is not without allure. He asks: If luck is random, why are we always bumping into this "spontaneous emergence of order from disorder"? He talks about a "library angel" that brings him good luck with research projects. Often, he says, he goes to a library in search of some obscure reference, expecting to spend hours or days on the hunt. Strolling along the shelves, he grabs a book at random. The book contains exactly the reference he wants. How does it happen? Something is synchronizing events in his life. His need for the reference and his random grab for the book are somehow made to converge, brought together by some force that "transcends mechanical causality."

Koestler asks: What is randomness anyway? Some kinds of events seem to happen more randomly at some times than at others. He tells of an odd and charming experiment involving "luck" and baby chicks. British scientists rigged up a heat lamp in such a way that it kept turning itself on and off in an uncontrolled, utterly random fashion. Probability law would predict that a device of this kind should behave like a tossed coin. Runs of one outcome or the other can be expected, but in the long run the total minutes of "off" and "on" should be just about equal. The heat lamp did, indeed, behave this way when it was sitting on a table by itself. But when the scientists put baby chicks in an enclosure beneath it, its behavior changed.

The chicks peeped miserably when it was off. They were too cold. They wanted it on. The only thing they could count on to bring them warmth was luck, and luck came to their aid. Whenever they were there, the device remained on for longer periods than off.

The chicks, in other words, had a run of apparently infallible good luck. The scientists concluded that something beyond ordinary randomness was at work. What was it? Psychic theorists would suggest telekinesis: the scientists willed the lamp to stay on because they were good-hearted fellows and also because they wanted their experiment to produce interesting results. Koestler and his scientific colleagues prefer to think some order-making force synchronized events in the chicks' favor.

Things aren't as random as they seem, the synchronists insist. There are underlying patterns, hidden forces quietly straining to make order out of chaos. If we want to understand luck, all we need to do is understand how the patterns work. . . .

Linda W., waitress. She is 46, slim. Her face is pretty, but there is weariness in it and in the way she walks and sits. I interview her in a bright, sunny room provided by an Alcoholics Anonymous group in New York. We drink coffee in plastic cups.

"You want to know about patterns?" she says. "Oh boy, you sure came to the right person. I've got this recurrent thing in my life. It's been hounding me since I was a kid, and I figure it will go on hounding me till I die. It's alcohol. That's my private devil: alcohol. Whenever I thought life was going to give me a break,

80

whenever I had something good going, then something bad would happen to smash it up. And the bad things, well, there would always be alcohol mixed up in it somewhere. I can't escape from it."

Linda was born in Cleveland. Her father, a business executive, was an alcoholic who enjoyed fair success in his career until he reached early middle age. Linda planned to go to college and study business administration. "But in my junior year of high school, the booze caught up with my dad. He began showing up at business conferences staggering drunk, and finally the company ran out of patience and fired him. He never got another good job as far as I know. He walked out on the family a while after that, and we never heard of him again until he turned up dead in some fleabag hotel in California."

There was no longer any money for college. Linda switched to typing and shorthand courses in her last year of high school, graduated, and went through a series of secretarial jobs. "I didn't like the work. It was boring and the pay was low. I finally landed a really neat job, secretary to the head of a little ad agency in Chicago. The pay was pretty good, but what I liked most was that they promised I wouldn't be stuck in that job. When I learned the ropes, they said they'd move me into more interesting work."

She was working late one night when her boss, fresh from the cocktail hour at a local pub, came back to the office and made a drunken pass at her and she slapped him. "Next morning when I came to work, I could see it was all finished. He was mad, embarrassed, probably afraid I'd tell his wife—you know, a plain unworkable situation. I said, 'What's going to happen?' He said he didn't think we could work together any more and I'd better leave. What else could I do? I left."

She found another secretarial job, and there she met a salesman named Ralph, fell in love with him and married him. "I was doing some drinking by this time—not a whole lot, but once in a while I'd get drunk, like at weekend parties. I didn't know it then, but this is the first sign of alcoholism. I liked getting high, liked it too much. Some people stop at that weekend-high stage if they have a rewarding life and good people around, and when Ralph came into my life I did stop there. We had a wonderful marriage. He got a sales job at a bigger company a few weeks after the wedding, and pretty soon he was getting promotions and moving up the ladder. We moved to New York, and then we bought a house in the suburbs the month I found I was pregnant. It was a girl, and we called her Elizabeth, or Beth for short. That was the happiest time of my life."

Ralph was killed while driving home from a sales trip. An oncoming car swerved into his lane and smashed into him headon. The other driver was drunk.

Linda moved into a small apartment and got a job as a cocktail waitress. "I had Beth to take care of, and I needed this kind of night job because the only babysitter I could afford was a highschool girl. The tips were good. I made just enough money to keep Beth and me going. But by this time I was hitting the bottle hard. I felt sick most of the time, and a lot of nights I'd show up for work late or wouldn't show up at all. I got fired from that job, found another one, got fired from that too. I finally went to some AA meetings, then dropped out and got drunk, then dropped back in again—you know, the usual alcoholic story. Then I finally hit bottom. I went on an all-night drunk and woke up next morning in a strange hotel room with a man I'd never seen before. I was terrified, and I went back to AA and sobered up for good."

For several years she worked as a coffee-shop waitress, then found a job in a hotel dining room, where the tips were higher. The employee turnover was rapid, and in two years she was one of the old-timers, highly regarded by the management and with a good chance of being made the hotel's assistant food manager. But then alcohol came crashing into her life one more time.

One exit from the dining room led down a flight of narrow stone steps to a below-ground shopping mall. She was on her way down there one night when a drunken man came reeling down behind her. "He was really pickled, mumbling to himself. He came up so close behind me that I could smell his breath, and he kept coming closer. I suddenly thought, 'Oh, my God, he's going too fast to stop!' "

He was falling, in fact. He fell against her. He was a heavy man, perhaps twice her weight, and her legs gave way. They crashed down the steps with him mainly on top.

"I think I passed out for a few seconds, because I can't remember actually hitting the floor. When I came to, he was gone and there was a woman running toward me. She tried to help me up, but I knew I was in bad trouble. One of my legs wouldn't move."

The leg was broken in two places. One break was such that it required a special setting technique using a steel rod inserted into the bone marrow. "It was six months before I could hobble around without crutches. I lived on unemployment for a while, then got a sit-down job in a department store billing office. That was a few years ago. Today I'm back waitressing in coffee houses again."

Linda sips her coffee pensively and smiles. "I'm not the self-pitying type," she says. "Life is tough for everybody, I know that. But this alcohol thi- 3—when is it going to leave me alone?"

"I wish I could tell you something useful," I reply. I tell her about some of the luck theories I have heard, including the synchronicity theory, which seems to intrigue her. I tell her that any run of good luck or bad luck can stop at any time, and maybe hers has already stopped. That seems to cheer her up.

When we part I say the only thing I can think of. I wish her good luck.

PART III

Speculations on the Nature of Luck: Some Occult and Mystical Tries

1.

Numbers

WILLIAM BARBER, CITIZEN of Pennsylvania, was born on April 7, 1911. Does anybody care? William Barber cares, of course, and it is reasonable to suppose his mother and father cared too. But the isolated fact that he was born on a certain day seems unremarkably by itself, for it confers no distinction on Bill Barber. Everybody was born on a certain day. Indeed, of all the approximately 50 million babies who came into the world in 1911, roughly one-365th of them—137,000 or so—were born on the same day as Bill Barber: 4/7/11. Another crop of 4/7/11 babies had appeared in 1811 and 1711, and again and again back through the centuries. Thus Barber of Pennsylvania is not unique in that respect. What makes his birth date interesting is that he is a devotee of a peculiar luck-control system known as numerology. He is also a student of baseball, football, and the stock market. He has combined these disparate elements into a stock-market prediction system that demonstrably hasn't failed since 1960 and that, he says, has helped make him rich.

Speculations: Occult and Mystical

As has happened before in this book and will no doubt happen again, I find myself in the embarrassing position of reporting events which, to my pragmatic and perhaps too-Western mind, have no apparent right to be true. How can numerology predict the course of the stock market, whose future is unpredictable to even the brightest analysts on Wall Street? What nonsense! And yet Bill Barber's irrational prediction system has worked without a hitch all through the 1960s and all through the 1970s so far. Why? What goes on? Is there something to this business of "lucky" numbers after all?

Who knows? Numerology, which calls itself a science but perhaps doesn't quite deserve to, is based on this very thesis: that there is a mysterious connecting link between numbers and the events in human life. If the numbers are lucky, the events will supposedly be lucky, and if not, not. Does that make sense? Well, no, not to everybody. But it is certainly not difficult to see why some people have become obsessed with numbers and have attributed magical or predictive powers to them.

We poor souls in this last half of the twentieth century flop and flounder daily in a great cold soup of numbers. We have telephone numbers, and Social Security numbers, and the national debt, and our personal debts, and a lot of other numbers, some of which we would like to forget but aren't allowed to. Moreover, numbers are often involved in the chances we take and in their lucky or unlucky outcomes. All gambling games are, of course, festooned with numbers. Lotteries, roulette, horses, dice, cards: numbers not only express the odds and the degree of victory or defeat, but are often printed on the very paraphernalia of the game. So it need not surprise us that there are people who, immersed in this gummy broth of numbers from which there is no escape, start to notice apparent connections and coincidences and end by believing in some kind of synchronicity.

Numbers

Bill Barber, a large, genial, white-haired fellow in his middle sixties, is such a man. Oddly, he is an accountant by profession: deals with numbers in nonoccult ways to earn his daily bread. Then again, perhaps that isn't odd after all. He is both accountant and numerologist because he is fascinated by the interplay of numbers, can't get enough of them. "I was a math whiz in school," he told me, "not because I was any brainier than other kids but because I took the trouble to learn the tricks, you know, the shortcuts. Numbers were my hobby. Along about age fifteen, I started to notice certain numbers kind of recurring in my life. Whenever something unexpected and good happened to me—a stroke of luck, you know—there those numbers would be. They were the numbers of my birthday, four, seven, and eleven. Those are *dandy* numbers!"

He told me this in a New York coffee shop one day when he was passing through the city. He drank tea and smoked a cigar. He had a big grin, a red face, and startlingly bright blue eyes. Obviously deriving huge enjoyment from his topic, he listed all the (to him) interesting properties of the three numbers. He pointed out that the first two numbers $4+7$, add up to the last, 11. I didn't quite understand the significance of this but it evidently pleased him because it indicated some kind of order, some mysterious interconnection. He pointed out that the three numbers $4+7+11$ add up to 22, the sum of whose digits is one of the lucky numbers, 4. And that if you multiply the numbers $4 \times 7 \times 11$, the result is 308, whose digits add up to 11. And that if you square the three numbers and multiply the squares, the result is 94,864, the sum of whose digits is 31, the sum of whose digits, in turn, is once again 4. And that . . .

Well, you get the point. To Bill Barber, those three numbers are terrific. They have a lot of properties that don't seem particularly useful but, to a numerologist, are significant in ways that can't quite be articulated.

I asked about his stock-market prediction system.

"Ah," he said, "that's a very interesting thing. I discovered it in 1964 and checked it back to 1960, and it has gone on working every year since, right up through 1975. It tells me whether the market will go up or down next year. It's infallible!"

Unarguably so, at least since 1960. I have checked it with skepticism and care. It would have produced wrong results several times in the 1950s, but not since. Anybody using it to time moves into and out of the market for the past decade and a half would have perceptibly increased his or her chances of winning. It is a three-step calculation, and it goes like this:

Step 1. Take the last digit of the current year. If it's 1974, you take the 4.

Step 2. Find out the results of the Rose Bowl football game at the start of the year. The game is always played on New Year's Day, and there is always somebody in every neighborhood and office who remembers the score. If the winner's score was 30 or over, add 1 to the year's last digit. Again taking 1974 as our example, we note that Ohio State flattened Southern California that year by a score of 42–21. And so, as the formula requires, we add 1 to the 4 of 1974, and it becomes a 5.

Step 3. Find out how many no-hit games were pitched in major league baseball during the year's regular season. The same sports statistician who remembered the Rose Bowl score will probably have this statistic, too, on the tip of his tongue. (Don't count incomplete games. The ones that count are the ones that went the full nine innings.) Add this number to the number you arrived at in step 2. In 1974 there were 2 no-hit games, so we add that to our 5 and end up with the number 7.

Prediction: If this final number is a 4, 7, or 11, the stock market will go up in the *following* year. If it is any other number, the market will go down.

As I said, I checked. I used *Standard & Poor's Composite Index* as the criterion of upness or downness on the market, and the *World Almanac* and *Reader's Di-*

gest Almanac gave me the necessary sports statistics. And sure enough . . .

Mad, you say. Perhaps. Yet it may be no madder than the approach of brokers, financial analysts, and other traditional Wall Street oracles. Their optimistic belief is that the market, though essentially an irrational engine, can be predicted by rational means. If Bill Barber is wrong, they are probably no righter. There is no rational way to predict the market. It is powered by emotion, not reason. The only certifiable way to win is to have good luck.

It is always a mistake to ignore or deny the luck component of a game, particularly when the component is large. Most professional Wall Streeters seem to do just this most of the time. They find it soothing to believe that the market's long-term future can be presaged by the diligent application of human reason. This gives them an illusion of preparedness and makes them feel good. Unfortunately, the result is that they keep coming up with predictions that sound more solid and reliable than they are. The predictions are, in fact, mere guesses, hardly more reliable than a guess you might make about future numbers on a roulette wheel.

The luckiest market players are those who recognize the market as at least partly a game of luck, not a game of pure reason. Clever reasoning can certainly help in stock speculation, but not in terms of far forecasts. It is doubtful that any Wall Street pro knows any more about the stock market's long-term future than do I or Bill Barber.

The fact is that Barber's guesses about the future have all been correct. He sold everything late in 1968 because his prediction number that year came out 13, indicating to him that 1969 would be a bad year to own stocks. O Lord, it surely was. In 1969 the number came out 15, indicating that 1970 would also be a gloomy year. It was. In 1970 the number was 4, presaging better times in 1971. Bill Barber bought some stocks early in 1971 and ended the year a little richer.

Before we go too far in praise of the Barber System, however, we had better bring some cleansing skepticism to bear. Barber thinks his system works because of some occult connection between his lucky numbers and the events they allegedly predict, and the evidence he offers is that things have turned out right 15 years in a row. But it is just as easy to believe (for me, I think, easier) that he is simply the beneficiary of an unusually long run of luck, like a run of fifteen wins in roulette. It is perfectly possible for random events to work in a given man's or woman's favor fifteen times in a row, though it doesn't happen often. However, there is no guarantee that the sixteenth turn of the wheel will also be favorable. Next year or the year after, some of Wall Street's rational prediction systems may produce a luckier hit than the Barber System.

Bill Barber's answer to this: "Sure, the system could go wrong in some years. It won't surprise me. I don't expect the system to be perfect. I only expect it to boost the odds in my favor—give me a right answer more often than I could get by chance. If I ever play roulette I'll put my money on 4, 7, and 11, but I won't expect those numbers to come up every time. I'll only look for them to come up a bit more often than the statistical odds say they should."

Has he ever played roulette?

"No, it looks like a boring game to me."

A casual cocktail-party survey reveals that about three out of four men and women, if asked what their lucky numbers are, will have an answer to give and will give it with a straight face. (We've already met Eric Leek, for instance, the New Jersey lottery winner who likes the number 10.) Among dedicated gamblers the ratio is much higher than three in four—so much higher that I would venture to say it approaches 99 in 100. But whether you enjoy gambling or not, the likelihood is that you identify a certain number, or perhaps more than one, as lucky for you. Perhaps you think of yourself as a coolly rational man or woman, not given to superstition. Still . . . there is that number, hovering somewhere in the murky depths of your consciousness, a number that has somehow become associated with happy events in your life.

Unlucky numbers are also common currency. Many people who claim to pooh-pooh other superstitions are markedly uncomfortable in the presence of the number 13, for instance. This gloom-shrouded number is regarded without enthusiasm in nearly all Western nations and in Soviet Russia. (Other nations have their own numerical phobias. In Japan, for example, there is felt to be something wrong with 4.) The fear of 13 is unaccountably strong in America, despite the fact that our nation enjoyed great good luck after starting out with 13 colonies, and despite the fact that our ubiquitous dollar bill has 13 all over it. If you examine the green side of a dollar bill you will see a pyramid with 13 steps, a shield with 13 stripes, a cluster of 13 stars, and an eagle with 13 tailfeathers which holds 13 arrows in one claw and a 13-leaved olive branch in the other. Is a dollar bill unlucky? Perhaps a ten-dollar bill is luckier, but few Americans would refuse a dollar— or even $13—if you thrust it on them.

Still, we avoid 13 when we can. Hosts and hostesses go to sometimes ridiculous lengths to have numbers other than 13 at dinner. Many buildings lack a designated 13th floor and many hotels have no rooms numbered 13. (In Japan, similar strange games are played in avoidance of 4.) Many Americans studiously avoid making any decisions or commitments, or embarking on new ventures, or as far as possible doing anything at all on Friday the 13th.

There have been courageous souls in our national past, as in all nations, who have scoffed at this triskaidekaphobia and have sought to prove 13 is an inoffensive and even amiable number after all. One such was Ralph Branca, pitcher for the Brooklyn Dodgers a quarter-century ago. Against the tremulous urgings of more superstitious teammates, Branca requested and got 13 as his playing number. He pitched a good workmanlike game all through 1951 and helped lift his team into a pennant playoff with the New York Giants. Until the last few seconds of the last playoff game, the Dodgers seemed to have the pennant in their pockets. But then disaster struck—disaster so sudden and of such stunning magnitude that baseball historians still talk of it in awed tones today.

Branca's Dodgers were ahead, and it was the last half of the ninth inning, and Branca was pitching. Two Giants were on base, but two were out. The very last Giant, Bobby Thomson, was at bat. All Branca needed to do was get this one man out, and the game and the pennant were his. The game was so obviously over that the crowd was already drifting to the exits, and millions of other fans were turning off their TV sets and radios and starting to see about collecting their bet money.

Then Branca threw everything away with a single unlucky pitch. He said later that it felt wrong even before the ball left his hand. Bobby Thomson hit a home run off that pitch, and the Giants took the pennant, and no Dodger either in Brooklyn or Los Angeles has ever since worn the number 13.

It seems odd that 13 is a bad-luck number to a large portion of the population, but no good-luck number has a following anywhere near that large. For reasons that have never been well explained, people are more independent in picking lucky numbers than in shying away from 13.

Some people adopt lucky numbers in a random way and, if asked what gives those numbers their peculiar luck-producing power, merely shrug and grin and offer no defense. Such a number might have become a man's or woman's pet in childhood or adolescence. It was the number worn on a football shirt in some bright sweet season, perhaps, or it was the street number of a house where good times were had, or it was the head count of members in a fondly remembered neighborhood gang.

Other people, like Bill Barber, pick their lucky numbers with more meticulous care and have some kind of rationale to offer—some reason or architecture of reasons why those numbers are better than other numbers. Such a rationale often depends on an appealing, but otherwise useless, set of properties or relationships among the numbers.

Bill Barber likes his numbers because adding and multiplying them in various ways produces pleasingly orderly results. The numbers look tidy. They appear cozy. They seem to belong together. My own pet numbers are 6 and 28, and I have an absolutely splendid rationale for this choice. For one thing, they are the numbers that express my birthday, June 28. For another thing, 6 and 28 are the only two "perfect" whole numbers below 100. In number theory, a perfect number is one that equals the sum of its factors. The factors of 6 are 1, 2, and 3, which add up to 6. The factors of 28 are 1, 2, 14, 4, and 7, which add up to 28. Perfect numbers are very rare. There are only a couple of dozen in the first million. You can see why I find my numbers dazzlingly attractive.

Do they do me any good? Probably not much. I once played roulette on a cruise ship, and I put my 25-cent chips on 6 and 28. If either number had come up it would have paid off at 35 to 1. That is, I would have received $8.75, plus my quarter back. But the odds against winning when you play two numbers that way on an American wheel are 19 to 1 on any given spin. I played 20 times, during which neither number came up and I lost $10. I quit, and the very next number to come up was a 6. Angry and morose, I left the casino and went off to have a drink. One of the other players later took the trouble to seek me out and tell me some more depressing news. During the dozen or so spins of the wheel after I left the table, 28 came up twice.

What should this have taught me? I suppose the lesson is that lucky numbers are fun to keep and coddle, but that you shouldn't expect too much of them. Just keep them around for, uh, good luck.

Nancy Berman, retired math teacher. She lives in California and visits Las Vegas for a couple of weeks every year. She claims that she nearly always goes home with more money than she brought. She likes blackjack, which has elements of both luck and skill, and she also likes roulette, a game of pure luck. She thinks her consistent good luck results partly from paying attention to a mysterious 11-digit number that she calls the Great Power Palindrome.

Skip lightly through the next few paragraphs if math bores you or makes you cry. A palindrome is a number or phrase whose front end is the mirror image of its rear end. It reads the same backward and forward, as "A man, a plan, a canal, Panama." A numerical palindrome would be a number such as 10101.

It turns out that some very pretty palindromes (pretty to a lover of numbers, that is) can be made by raising groups of consecutive numbers to various powers. If you take all the numbers from 0 to 10 and square them (multiply each by itself, as 2×2), the last digits of the resulting square numbers will line up in order like this: 01496569410. Lovely and mysterious. You get the same last-digit palindrome when you square the numbers from 10 to 20, and from 20 to 30, and so on for all eternity.

Cubing consecutive numbers in the same way produces another endlessly repeated number that is interesting for different reasons but isn't a palindrome, and so does raising consecutive numbers to the fifty power. Nancy Berman's Great Power Palindrome comes from raising the numbers to the fourth power (as $2 \times 2 \times 2 \times 2$). When you do that, you get endless repetitions of this charming lineup: 01616561610.

Raising numbers to still higher powers produces

nothing new. You get the same palindromes and other repeating numbers all over again. Thus, in Nancy Berman's terminology, the fourth-power palindrome is the "highest." That is what entitles it to be called Great. Besides, it looks good and is easy to remember.

But of what earthly use is it? Nancy Berman believes the four numbers of which the Great Power Palindrome is built—0, 1, 5, and 6—have a powerful and occult affinity for one another. When any one of them turns up on a roulette wheel, she holds, the other three strive energetically to turn up shortly afterward. "My method is to watch a wheel without playing. I wait until one of the four numbers comes up. When it does, I immediately bet the other three numbers. At least one of them is almost certain to come sooner than the odds would predict."

Strange. Nancy Berman is a tall woman with gray hair, a bright mind, a direct gaze, and a handshake stronger than most men's. There is nothing in her look or manner that would suggest any intellectual softness, any gullibility, any mystical vagueness. She herself recognizes that this Great Power Palindrome business is not in harmony with her basic nature. "I'm a very practical woman," she says, with a faintly puzzled look on her face. "I don't believe what I can't see, especially when my own money is involved. I don't read my horoscope in the paper or carry a luck charm around. Frankly, I feel kind of embarrassed about this numerology thing. If you want to argue with me about it, I won't argue, I won't try to defend it. But—"

But what? Perhaps what it boils down to is that a lucky number, if you have one, can give you comfort. It can guide your actions in a baffling situation where there are many choices to make but no rational basis for choosing. The game of roulette is certainly such a situation. There is no rational approach that will improve your chances of winning. Certain types of bets and certain betting systems will slow down the speed with which you lose your money, but beyond that there are no rational choices to make. One number is as good as another. Facing this kind of situation, with many open choices but no reasonable criteria of choice, you might simply stand there paralyzed, unable to make any choice at all.

Paralysis of will is not of great importance around a roulette table, of course. It means simply that you never get into the game. But in other areas of life, more meaningful areas in which choices must be made with insufficient or nonexistent data, paralysis of will can be decidedly harmful. There are situations in which you must do *something*, thought there is no good way to choose among several somethings. If you're driving down an unfamiliar highway and come to a fork and have no idea which route to take, you must make an irrational choice and make it fast. If you stop your car in the middle of the road and sit there paralyzed, you put yourself in mortal peril. In such a situation, anything that helps you make a choice is a thing to be valued. *Anything*, including a lucky number.

Nancy Berman feels her Great Power Palindrome makes sense from this point of view, at least. "Whether you believe the numbers have any special powers or not," she says, "the plain fact is that I wouldn't play roulette at all if I didn't have something like this to guide me. I wouldn't know how to make the choices. Numerology may sound dumb to a lot of people, but it gets me into a game I enjoy. I'd enjoy the game even if I lost a lot of the time. What makes it more enjoyable and surprising to me is that I mostly win." She smiles and adds, "But you don't have to believe that, of course."

Well, I don't know whether I believe it or not. Perhaps most of her Las Vegas winnings come from blackjack, a game in which clever and rational choices can appreciably increase the odds in a player's favor. As for roulette, we've already noted that the First Law of Probability is "anything can happen," and the Second Law is "if it can happen, it will." Long runs of luck, even lifelong runs, do happen sometimes. Some of us might not be prepared to believe Nancy Berman's roulette success comes from mysterious forces operating through the Great Power Palindrome, but we can at least allow the possibility of coincidence. It may be that the 0, 1, 5, and 6 just happen to have come up a lot whenever Nancy Berman has turned up near a roulette wheel.

No matter what we believe or how we interpret her story, it seems undeniable that what she says about choice-making is sensible. Lucky people as a breed are notably gifted with this ability to make choices in the face of inadequate data, and later we will probe this interesting proposition more deeply.

Harold Muhs, retired bartender. He lives in Trenton, New Jersey. He is 69, a friendly but not talkative man. Like many bartenders he keeps most of his thoughts to himself, including thoughts about luck. Other people, however, have done a good deal of talking and thinking about him in recent years, for fortune has lifted him out of the tranquil obscurity that he often thinks he would have preferred.

On January 4, 1973, he won $50,000 in the New Jersey State lottery. On March 4, 1976, he won again: this time $250,000.

His preliminary "post position" in the 1976 drawing was 4. The fact, and the fact that both big wins occurred on the fourth day of a month, have attracted the eager attention of numerologists in his vicinity. Some of them, and also some synchronists, have gone to extravagant lengths to demonstrate relationships between various numbers and Harold Muhs. They point out that some alluringly orderly results can be obtained by multiplying the digits of those two dates, 1/4/73 and 3/4/76. Multiplying $1 \times 4 \times 7 \times 3$ produces 84 while the digits of the other date produce 504. Not only is 84 a factor of 504, but both numbers end in 4 and are divisible by 4. Furthermore, if you multiply 84

× 504, or if you square 84, or if you square 504, in all three cases you get a number whose digits add up to the same number, 18. It seems like a neat case of numerical synchronicity.

"Well, Mr. Muhs," I ask, "what do you think of all this numerological stuff? Do you think the number four has some kind of magic affinity for you? Or the number eighteen, maybe?"

"Nope. Only number I'm interested in is three."

"Oh? Why three?"

"I'm waiting to see if lightning will strike the same place a third time."

2.

Destiny and God

SOME PEOPLE BELIEVE there is a God, while others do not, and still others are not sure. Among those who believe such a being exists, there are hundreds of theories—perhaps thousands—about the nature of this being and his relationship to us poor mortals on earth. But in terms of luck, the believers can be said to fall into two large groups.

One group holds that, though God created us and has some general interest in our welfare, he makes no attempt to exert detailed control over our individual lives. He is fond of the human race at large but doesn't specifically worry about the outcome of your life or mine. In this theory, we are put on earth to struggle along on our own, find our own luck, hack our way to our own dim destinies with neither help nor hindrance from above.

The second group of believers, perhaps larger, holds that God does concern himself with each individual life. He puts each of us on earth for some purpose of his own and carefully manipulates each life so that the purpose will be properly accomplished. When you were born, this theory contends, God already knew what he wanted you to do with your life and what your destiny was to be. Whatever has happened to you since then was part of his plan. Luck, in other words, is God's will.

This second view may be the most widely held luck theory of all. It would be presumptuous to attempt an analysis of the theory here, and it would also be superfluous, for the number of books that have been written about God and human destiny must already approach a million. Prominent among them is the Bible. The Bible never says in so many words, "Luck is God's will," but that is one of its essential meanings. What is said in the Bible has never been said quite so well anywhere else, though many have tried. I am not about to try.

Let's content ourselves with talking to one remarkable woman who espouses the theory that luck is God's will. Like all the other stories we have encountered in the book, her story is told here for purposes of information, not advocacy. If you hold a different theory about luck, this story is not likely to change your mind. What it will do, if it does its job adequately, is to explain why some men and women find it reasonable to believe that an unseen intelligence controls all the details of their destinies.

A word about language before we go on. This unseen and unknown intelligence goes by many names. I will use the Christian and Jewish word "God" because it is a nice short word and expresses the meaning well enough for most purposes. I will also use the classical designation "he," though obviously this mysterious being that few of us have ever met in person could just as easily be "she" or "it" or even "they." The word "he" is a stylistic convenience, not a sexist comment nor an attempt to deny the possibility of a God Group. And to avoid tripping over ponderous pronouns, I won't follow the exaggeratedly pious style of capitalizing "he" and "him." If there is a God, and if he reads books, and if he is as benevolent as his worshipers say, he is more likely to be amused by this than offended.

Irene Kampen, author. She is perhaps best known for *Life Without George,* a warm and funny book on which the Lucille Ball television show was based. She has written several other books, all characterized by the same wry humor, all drawn from her experiences as a middle-class suburban woman trying to hold her own in a confusing and not always friendly world. She has a loyal following of readers. Her books and the TV show have made her fairly wealthy. She has done a good deal of thinking about this fame and fortune, for it came to her suddenly and unexpectedly in middle age. Before it came, she was in a pit of despair so black that there seemed to be no way out.

"If somebody had come up to me in 1960 and predicted that I was going to write books," she says. "I would have said, 'Ridiculous.' I had no thought of writing any book. And if that same person had predicted I would be a successful Author with a capital 'A,' I would have laughed out loud. I was divorced, broke, trying to raise a child. I was utterly miserable. There was nowhere to turn. Life seemed to be over for me. But then—"

But then came luck. Colossal strokes of it, a whole series of them, smashing into her life as though from nowhere. When the dust cleared, the entire course of that life was drastically changed.

Luck? Irene Kampen believes it was all planned from the beginning by God. "I was put on earth to make people laugh," she says, in a tone of absolute conviction. "Everything that has happened to me, including all that misery and suffering, was designed to bring this about. I am where I am today because God arranged it. I can't see how any other explanation is possible. In order for this drastic change to have happened in my life, hundreds of separate events had to happen to just the right people in just the right ways at just the right times. These events had to fit together like pieces of a puzzle. If *one piece* has been missing, the whole thing would have collapsed, the process would have stopped, and today I'd still be stuck where I was in 1960. I've got to believe a higher power arranged it."

Irene Kampen, in her middle fifties, is a woman of great grace and extraordinary wit. If it is true that God put her here to make people laugh, she is serving him well. In and around Ridgefield, Connecticut, where she lives, she is among the most popular speakers at Lions Club meetings, Women's Club Lunches, Rotary dinners. She frequently tours the rest of the country to speak before other groups. Her audiences almost always leave grinning. She denies that she possessed this talent when she was younger. The ability to make people laugh—the quality of dry, self-joshing wit that is especially hers—was created and nurtured in her, she believes, by the same supreme planner who manipulated her into the position of Author. She feels her life was engineered from the beginning so that, when she became a writer of books, she would be equipped with two necessities: a lode of experience to write about, and a character so shaped by events that the writing would be funny.

Irene Kampen was born in Brooklyn. Her childhood was happy and relatively uneventful. She studied journalism at the University of Wisconsin—a university she chose by what she thought was a random process. She now feels the choice was guided with care from above. At Wisconsin she met the young man who was to become her husband. The Second World War was raging at the time, and he enlisted as a bomber pilot. She worked briefly at a newspaper job while waiting for him to return, didn't like the work, and quit. The bomber pilot returned and took up his interrupted career as an illustrator. He and Irene were married. They bought a house in Levittown, Long Island. A daughter was born.

"This was a happy period of my life," she recalls. "I was a young suburban mother, full-time. In those days you could be a young suburban mother without feeling you had to make excuses for enjoying it. I thought it was grand."

Destiny was already in motion, however. Her parents bought a home in Ridgefield. Irene and her husband visited from time to time, liked the small New England town (today a large New England town), and eventually decided to settle there too. Her husband by this time was doing well in his career. They could afford to have a house designed for them by an architect.

"The architect and his wife were a friendly couple. When we finished talking shop the four of us would often go out together for a social evening. After a while it developed that the architect's wife and my husband were talking about a lot of things besides shop. They ran off together."

After two years of separation Irene and her husband were divorced. She kept the house in Ridgefield. To support herself and her daughter she went to work in her father's florist shop in New York. That hardly covered expenses. To help maintain the house and also because she was lonely, she invited a friend to move in with her. The friend was another divorced Ridgefield woman with a little boy.

This period was the bottom of Irene Kampen's life. "The only thing I had to live for was my daughter. If it hadn't been for her. . . . Well, anyway, it was in this dark time, the late 1950s, that I started going to church. I hadn't been seriously interested in religion before, but now I was desperate for any comfort I could get. I didn't pray for things to get better. I was too pessimistic for that. My prayer was: 'I know I'm finished and I'm not asking for any fairy-tale surprises. Just, please, don't let things get any worse.' "

She did not know that a distant engine of fate was

already beginning a slow, ponderous turn in her direction. Across the continent in California, the often stormy marriage and business partnership of Lucille Ball and Desi Arnaz was breaking up. Irene recalls reading the story in a magazine or newspaper. She felt a brief pang of sympathy for the copper-haired actress and then, of course, forgot all about her.

One day Irene happened to meet Karl Nash, editor and publisher of the weekly Ridgefield *Press*. Nash remarked that he was troubled by a lack of humor in his newspaper. Irene had done no writing since her brief journalistic venture before marriage, and until this chance meeting with Karl Nash the idea of resuming that aborted career had never occurred to her. She now believes God deliberately brought about her meeting with the publisher. She went home that night, thought about what Nash had said, and returned to him a few days later with the proposal that she write a humorous weekly column about local events and people. Nash looked at some samples she had written, liked them, and offered her $5 a week to continue. "That wasn't a lot of money," she says, "but in my financial condition I couldn't afford to turn anything down." The column, entitled "The Thursday Thing," ran for a few months. Then Nash began to receive complaints from certain local personages whom the column had twitted and who were not amused. "The Thursday Thing" was dropped.

The next two moves in God's mysterious manipulation occurred one day at the local library. Irene went there to return a book. On the way in she met an acquaintance, an artist. He offered his opinion that "The Thursday Thing" had been excellent, that it was a shame the columns had been stopped, and that Irene ought to gather them into a book. Irene said thank you but doubted the wisdom of the advice.

She went into the library to return her book. It was a book of alleged humor written by a woman, but Irene had not found it very funny. She said so to the librarian. She added, "I could write a funnier book than that."

The librarian was evidently in a prickly mood that day. Librarians often hear comments like Irene's—"I could write a better book"—and usually they nod politely and keep their thoughts to themselves. This librarian, however, felt the need to get something off her chest. She sharply suggested that Irene Kampen put her typewriter where her mouth was. "It's easy to say you can write a book," said the librarian. "People come in here and say it every week. Once, just once, I'd like to meet somebody who not only says it but does it."

Irene had been encouraged by the artist's words and then, minutes later, stung by the librarian's. The combination was powerful. Gears started to mesh inside her. That night she began a book about the experiences of two divorced women living in a house with two kids. She worked on it in free time over the next year or so, with no sense of hurry and no idea of what she would do with it. "I didn't even know why I was writing it," she says. "It was more or less a hobby, something to keep my mind off my troubles. I guess I must have dreamed about getting it published, but I didn't seriously believe that would ever happen. I just went on writing it without thinking beyond the next page. It was a funny kind of urge . . . I couldn't explain it then, but I think I can now. The urge came from—somewhere beyond me. It was part of the plan."

The next element in this delicately constructed plan was a seemingly accidental meeting in New York. "I was on my way to catch a train home when I bumped into an old friend I hadn't seen for years, a TV writer. If I hadn't met him, everything would have gone down the drain. The meeting was an essential piece of the puzzle. He bought me a drink. I told him what I'd been doing with myself, and the upshot was that I gave him a copy of my unfinished book and he showed it to a TV script editor. They thought it needed more work and made some suggestions for improving it, especially in terms of organization. So over the next few months I tinkered with it and rearranged it."

If God's plan were to go on working, it was essential that this better-arranged book be in existence as the next phase went into operation. This phase had begun when Cyril Ritchard, the actor, moved to Ridgefield. First Irene's mother and then Irene got to know him. At a weekend party in Ritchard's house, Irene met a Hollywood writer. "I told him, 'I've got something I'm working on. I think it's a book.' He wouldn't have been much interested if I'd just said I was *going* to write a book. But since I had an actual manuscript to show him, he was polite enough to say he'd like to see it."

He liked it. He showed it to a Twentieth Century-Fox story editor. She thought she liked it but wasn't sure. She suggested that it be sent to a New York literary agent she knew.

The agent would probably not have read it if it had simply come over the transom from an unknown woman in the suburbs. But since it came with a recommendation from a prominent editor, the agent read it, found it promising, and submitted it to a publisher. The publisher liked it and offered a $1,000 advance and a standard royalty contract.

"I was overwhelmed," says Irene. "To me, back then, a thousand dollars was a fortune. I would have been happy just to have somebody publish the book, but to have them actually give me money in advance—this was fantastic!"

Her agent was less enthusiastic. An advance of $1,000 is quite parsimonious. In offering it, the publisher's editors were saying tacitly that they didn't really expect to sell many copies of the book. More to save face than for any other reason, the agent asked for a few changes in the contract. One requested change provided that, in the event any part of the book was sold to TV, all earnings from that source would go to the author. The publisher, no doubt chuckling over this fantasy, amiably agreed. "It was obviously ridiculous to dream about TV back then," Irene concedes. "Frankly, I was amused myself."

Out in California, however, Lucille Ball and Desi Arnaz were grumpily parted. The somewhat soured actress was looking for a new "vehicle," as they say in TV-land. She and her friend, Vivian Vance, wanted to find some kind of situation comedy in which there were no prominent roles for men. They had been hunting for about three years and were growing desperate.

One day Lucille Ball's agent picked up a copy of Irene Kampen's book.

The show ran for seven years and is still appearing in reruns today.

As is true of any other story about luck, the interpretation is not fixed. It would be perfectly possible to retell Irene Kampen's story from the viewpoint of randomness, astrology, psi forces, or any other theory. She herself admits this—but only reluctantly and only sometimes. To her, the religious interpretation is as real as are the facts of the story themselves.

Perhaps your own interpretation differs, and perhaps you are just as sure you are right. That is fine. However, don't waste time trying to sell your interpretation to anybody else. The only men and women who will listen to you will be those who already believe what you believe. Once people have reached conclusions about the nature of luck—even vague conclusions—they hardly ever change their minds.

3.

Charms, Signs, and Portents

MY FATHER USED to tell a story about causes and effects. Every day at precisely noon a fellow turns up on a busy street corner with a green flag and a bugle. He waves the flag, blows a few notes on the bugle, utters a mysterious incantation, and goes away. A cop, observing this exercise over a period of weeks, finally gets overwhelmed by curiosity. "What the *hell* are you doing?" asks the cop. "Keeping giraffes away," says the fellow. The cop says, "But there are no giraffes around here." The fellow says, "Doing a good job, ain't I?"

The characters in this story changed over the years, and often there were ribald elements in it, but the point was always the same. My father told it to refute what he called "silly damned superstitions," in which category he included all occult and mystical beliefs about luck. He was a Swiss banker, a man solidly rooted in the pragmatic industrial culture of Western Europe and America. If he could not actually see a cause operating to produce an effect—if he couldn't see precisely how the two were linked in terms of known physical laws—he doubted that any link existed.

And so he told the giraffe story whenever anybody tried to offer evidence in support of astrology: "My horoscope predicted exactly what would happen to me this week!" Or lucky numbers: "See, what did I tell you? I knew it would turn out fine because today is the sixth of the month!" Or Tarot cards, tea leaves, black cats, ladders, spilled salt, broken mirrors, rabbits' feet, or any of the hundreds of other things that are alleged to predict or influence luck.

The point of the story was unarguably sensible, of course. It is a logical fallacy to infer a cause-and-effect relationship from mere proximity. When two events happen simultaneously or consecutively, it may or may not be true that one is the cause of the other. If a black cat crossed your path last week and you broke your leg this week, it may be unjust to blame the cat.

On the other hand . . . who knows? It may be just as bad a fallacy to deny the existence of a causal link only because you can't see it. Devotees of astrology and other occult and mystical beliefs regard this thought as a main supporting pillar of their various rationales. They charge that our hard, practical, thing-oriented culture grants too little room to anything that can't be weighed, measured, or analyzed in a computer. "Just because a thing can't be explained in terms of your materialistic Western science," they say, "that's no reason to . . ."

They quote Hamlet a lot. Hamlet said: "There are more things in heaven and earth, Horatio, than are dreamt of in your philosophy." Hamlet was trying to tell his friend that he had just had a long conversation with a ghost. Those who use this overused quotation as a debating weapon, however, usually neglect to add that Horatio was not quite convinced. He leaned to a less occult theory: that Hamlet was probably crazy.

Hamlet and Horatio were entitled each to his own interpretation of events, and so was my father, and so

were all who argued with him, and so are you and I.
One good thing about occult and mystical explanations
of luck is that they are often interesting whether or not
you believe in them. They are also hopeful, for they
suggest the possibility of predicting or controlling one's
luck—or, perhaps better, having it controlled in one's
favor by a benevolent power such as God or a lucky
number. We've heard stories about God and numbers.
Let's look briefly at some other commonly held mystical beliefs.

Astrology is the science (or faith: choose your
word) which holds that human affairs are influenced
by the positions, movements, and relationships of the
sun, moon, stars, and planets. "If you can see a star,"
says Joseph Goodavage, an astrologer of some renown,
"then obviously its light is reaching you, its radiation.
If its radiation is impinging on you, then conceivably it
is influencing you in some way. Influencing you how?
That we don't know, any more than we know exactly
how the force of gravity works. But we can observe
and catalog the effects, and that is what astrologers
have been doing for thousands of years. Astrology is
an empirical science. We know, by observation, that a
certain pattern in the sky will produce certain effects in
people's lives on earth."

Some would charge Goodavage and his stargazing
colleagues with the logical sin of selecting evidence.
Astrologers hold, for example, that men and women
born under the sun sign of Cancer will tend to be alike
in certain respects. To prove the point they will offer a
list of Cancerians who display the correct characteristics. Their dossier of evidence does not include (1)
Cancer-born people who aren't like that, or (2) Scor-
pio-born people who are. So say the skeptics. Goodavage's reply is that the skeptics have studied the
problem in too superficial a way or haven't studied it at
all. If a Cancer-born man deviates in personality and
life pattern from the normal Cancer model, the obvious

reason (obvious to astrologers, that is) will turn out to be that the man's sun sign is not the strongest influence at work in his case. Perhaps the positions of the moon and Saturn were more important at his hour and place of birth.

Another well-known astrologer, Madeleine Monnet, made a simple suggestion when I took my question to her. "Try it," she said. "You don't have to give it a lifelong test, just a fair one. You'll see. It will work."

Shortly thereafter my wife, Dorothy, and I saw an intriguing ad in a newspaper. It offered something called a "Life-Luck Horoscope . . . The Secret of Having Good Luck." According to the ad, this new kind of horoscope had been developed by an organization calling itself the International Astrological Association (IAA), based in Canton, Ohio. IAA's chief astrologer was introduced as a woman named Cary Franks, whose nickname (the ad said) was Lady Luck. The price of the Life-Luck Horoscope was ten bucks.

Dorothy sent off a check, along with particulars about her hour and place of birth. Lady Luck sent back a 30-page booklet telling Dorothy much more than she wanted to know about her lucky years, days, hours, colors, numbers, "areas of association," and other matters. It was complicated. One point that seemed to stand out, however, was that a period of unusually good luck was approaching in Dorothy's life. The period spanned the late spring and early summer of 1976.

"We'll get rich!" I said. I urged her to buy a bundle of state lottery tickets. She did. They did not win us a nickel.

Nor did anything else particularly lucky happen as the allegedly blessed period continued. In fact, Dorothy was struck by a piece of maddening bad luck on a day when this streak of good fortune was supposed to be at its peak. She had recently returned to college, to complete an education that was interrupted years ago. On this purportedly lucky day she was scheduled to take a final exam in mathematics, the one subject she hates and fears. The time alloted for the exam was two hours. When she received her exam sheaf and discovered that it was 16 pages long, she panicked. In her hurry to finish before the time ran out, she made mistakes on problems that she could have handled easily at a more leisurely pace. Only when she got past page 8 did she realize that fate had played a cruel trick on her. Page 8 was the last page. She had received two exam sheafs stapled together.

I talked to some astrology enthusiasts about this. They scolded me for projecting my own unwarranted assumptions and expectations into Lady Luck's prediction. Lady Luck had predicted that the blessed period would be lucky, but she hadn't said what form the luck would take. She hadn't promised that Dorothy would win a lot of money in a lottery, nor that college exams would go smoothly. "Just wait and see," the stargazers said. "Before the period ends, there will be good luck in some form. It will probably be a form you don't expect."

They were right. Two similar and fairly remarkable events happened in close succession. Both had to do with money lost and found.

The first episode took place a few days after that ill-fated math exam. Dorothy was sitting on some steps outside one of the college buildings, waiting for a friend. The friend was delayed, so Dorothy began to read a book. It was a windy afternoon. The air was full of dead leaves, scraps of paper, and other flying debris. Dorothy was absorbed in her book and paid little attention to any of this until something struck her in the face. She tried to brush it away but the wind held it there. She pulled it off her cheek and looked at it. It was a twenty-dollar bill.

Suddenly she became aware that she was sitting in a snowstorm of money. Twenties, tens, ones: they were flying through the air, rustling around the steps and along the ground, plastered against walls and bushes.

She leaped up and began gathering them. As she chased and stamped and snatched, she kept looking around for some clue as to where this extravagant blizzard might have originated, but nobody else was in sight.

Finally she could see no more money on the loose. As she stood there with two handfuls of green paper, wondering what to do next, a frightened-looking girl stepped out of the building. The girl's eyes widened when she saw Dorothy standing baffled at the bottom of the steps.

"Is that your money?" the girl asked. Her voice quavered, as though tears were not far away.

Dorothy said no, she had just found the money blowing around.

The girl said, "Oh, thank God!" Her knees buckled and she sat on the steps, weak with relief.

It was not her money. It had been collected from sales of tickets to a class banquet. She had been on her way to deliver it to the office that was to handle the arrangements. She had put it in the pocket of her jeans. When she had arrived at the office a few minutes ago, she had found to her horror that more than half the money had somehow fallen out of her pocket.

"I don't know how I could ever have replaced it," she told Dorothy, "I'm just barely paying my bills as it is. Oh, I hope you picked up most of it."

"How much are you missing?" Dorothy asked.

"Exactly a hundred and twenty-two dollars," the girl said.

They counted the money in Dorothy's hand. The amount was $122. She had retrieved every last dollar.

Thus—something that Lady Luck's forecast didn't say specifically—Dorothy became an instrument of somebody else's rare good luck. This was translated into a fine windfall for Dorothy. The smile on the girl's face was worth much.

The second episode was the mirror-image of the first. Our family stopped one afternoon at one of those franchised roadside ice-cream places, a member of the Carvel chain. It had been a hot summer day, and the place was crowded with people of all ages, sizes, and (one presumes) degrees of honesty. Without knowing it, Dorothy dropped her wallet from her handbag. The wallet contained about $90 in cash, plus her driver's license, credit cards, and other valuable scraps of paper and plastic.

She discovered the loss the next day. When we went back to Carvel's, the manager calmly handed the full wallet back to her.

Apparently a quite surprising sequence of events had taken place. Many people had handled this wallet, and each of them had had an open opportunity to walk off with it or extract the contents. None had done so. It had been spotted on the ground by a youngster. He had handed it to his mother. She had given it to one of the teenage girls working behind the counter. That girl had put it on a shelf. Somebody else had moved it to a different place. Still another worker had turned it over to the manager. Nobody had taken a dollar.

Dorothy was so happy that she took the Carvel people a bottle of champagne. I wondered whether we should also send one to Lady Luck, by way of apologizing for our earlier sour assessment of her forecast. It seemed like a good idea for a while. But then, somewhere in the back of my head, I heard my father talking about giraffes.

Dreams are thought by some to hold information about the future—signs and portents which, if duly recognized and acted upon, can help the dreamer control the otherwise uncontrollable. There are people who believe dreams have helped them win lotteries and horse wagers, make correct business decisions, meet the right marital partners, find lost valuables and lost people, stay off ships that were about to sink and airplanes that were about to crash.

Dreams generally seem to consist of nonsense, so it

116

is probably not surprising that a great deal of nonsense has been written about them. It shows up in all kinds of places, from the journals of weird mystical cults to those of psychoanalysts. Worse, much of it is boring nonsense, for few things are less interesting than the narrative of somebody else's dream. Still worse, it is a type of material that can be shot through with inaccuracies and outright lies, none of them checkable. If somebody says, "I didn't sail on the *Titanic* because of a dream about drowning," there is no way to find out for certain whether the alleged dream actually occurred. A dream never leaves behind any factual evidence of its existence. You can only take the word of the dreamer—and since some people are very, very proud of their dreams, taking their word may not always be entirely prudent.

And so I've preferred to talk with people who have no wish or need to prove anything about those strange, irrational adventures that visit us when we sleep. One such man is Charles Kellner of Hillsdale, New Jersey, a retired sheet-metal craftsman who now works as a bartender. Charlie Kellner is an easygoing, amiable man in his middle fifties. He likes to work at bars where sports buffs and wagerers hang out because he is an enthusiastic collector of luck stories. He nurses no pet superstitions of his own, but he doesn't reject occult beliefs either. When a seemingly occult adventure happens to him, he treasures it as a story to be told but makes no attempt to recruit believers. He tells it with a grin, genially inviting his hearers to laugh at him and indeed leaving them unsure of whether he is laughing at himself.

He tells an intriguing story about dreams. "Luck seems to come in cycles with me," he says. "There'll be a time of bad luck and a time of good luck. Not only does the luck come in cycles, but so do the things— you know, the superstitious ideas—that seem to be connected with it. Like, take dreams. I've met a lot of horse players and other people who say their dreams tell them what to bet on, but I've never paid any attention to my own dreams or found them useful—except for one month last year. That month I suddenly found myself in the dream business. It had never happened before and it hasn't happened since, but that month was crazy. That month I made more money per hour by dreaming than I ever had by working. My wife said maybe I should stay asleep all the time. . . ."

It began with a dream about a haunted house. Dreams are seldom logical, and this one was no exception. Charlie Kellner had bought the house and was proudly showing a group of friends through it. They didn't like it and were telling him he was a fool to buy it. He wanted to show them he wasn't scared. For some reason that the dream plot did not make clear, it seemed to him that he could demonstrate cool nonchalance by stepping out the front door and reading off the house number in a loud voice. It was a three-digit number, 283. He stood in front of the house and bravely shouted the number up and down the street.

On awakening he found the number lodged in his mind. As far as he could recall, it was not a number that had ever been significant to him. It appeared to be just a random collection of three digits put together by his sleeping brain. It stayed with him all day, and it was still there when he went to buy his customary 50-cent ticket in New Jersey's "Pick-It" numbers game.

In playing Pick-It, you guess at a three-digit number. There are various prizes for making partially correct guesses. The big prize goes to those who guess all three digits in the correct order.

Charlie Kellner placed his bet on 283. "I had no faith in the dream," he says, "no superstitious notions or anything like that. But when you're playing one of these numbers games, one guess is as good as another. I figure you might as well have some fun and bet on numbers that have some kind of meaning to you—you know, even a crazy meaning." The number 283 was the winner, and the state of New Jersey handed Charlie $500.

A few nights later he had a vivid dream about his mother, who had died years before. When he went to buy his lottery ticket the following day he thought it would be fun to bet on his mother's old house number, 539. The number won him another $500.

And so it went. Dreams on subsequent nights turned up winning two-digit numbers. "I was bankrupting the state!" Charlie says.

Then the mysterious dreaming talent vanished as suddenly as it had arrived. Charlie has not since had another dream that did anything useful for him. "Whatever it was, it's gone," he says cheerfully. "Matter of fact, it even turned against me. Couple of months ago I had a dream about a building I once worked in. The building had a three-digit number that I saw clearly in my dream, so I bet on it the next day. Well, not only did I lose my fifty cents, but I found I'd remembered the number wrong. And even if I'd remembered it right, I still would have lost. It just goes to show you—"

He pauses and sits for a while, puzzling. "Well," he says finally, "I don't know what it goes to show you."

❀ PART IV ❀

The
Luck Adjustment

Introduction

AND NOW WE come to the core of our quest. We have worked our way into this labyrinth by many strange and twisted paths, and we stand finally at the center where the last mystery is kept. We are prepared to ask: How can we change our luck?

As we have seen, there are many theories about luck and how to handle it. Each theory makes sense to some people but not to others. Even the randomness theory, with its august sound of respectable science, is still only a theory. Its often assertive disciples insist that what they say is obviously and demonstrably true, but there is no way in which its precepts can be proven. All theories are alike in this respect: none can be proven to anybody who chooses to believe something else.

We have looked at some of the most commonly held theories without insisting that any choice be made among them. Each theory has been presented in its own best light, within the obvious limitations of available space. Each has been explained and justified by some of its more articulate disciples. It is unlikely that your personal views of luck have been changed radically since you started the book, for it was never the book's purpose to be argumentative or to push one theory at the expense of others. Perhaps some of your preexisting views have been reinforced or perhaps some new avenues of thought have been suggested to you. No matter. Whatever you believe, go on believing it. Whatever you want to explore, explore it. You are not about to be asked to change your views.

The Luck Adjustment is intended to supplement, not supplant, any theory of luck. It can work for you whether you believe in randomness, in mystic omens, or in anything else. It is not in itself a theory so much as a set of observations.

The observations are derived from a question: What do lucky people do that unlucky people don't do? I have applied this question to so many men and women in the past twenty years that I long ago lost count of them. The number is certainly over a thousand, which would make it a fair statistical sample. I have checked my observations with those of psychiatrists, gamblers, speculators, and other people who can be assumed to have some special knowledge of the subject or to have done more than the average amount of thinking about it. Each of these people bases observations on his or her own informal, specialized sample—in a psychiatrist's case, for instance, a sample of patients who have paraded through the office; in a gambler's case, a sample of remembered winners and losers.

It turns out that there are five outstanding characteristics that distinguish the lucky from the unlucky. These five characteristics—attitudes toward life and other people, internal psychological manipulations, ways of talking to oneself—turn up again and again in the stories of men and women who seem to enjoy consistent good luck. They are conspicuously absent in the stories of the unlucky. These are the five components of the Luck Adjustment.

1.

The Spiderweb Structure

A SPIDER STRINGS many lines to catch passing flies, and the bigger her web, the better she eats. So it is with those who would catch good luck. In general, and with exceptions, the luckiest men and women are those who have taken the trouble to form a great many friendly contacts with other people.

Let's see why this is so and how the spiderweb structure works.

O. William Battalia is an instrument of luck. It is his business and in most cases his pleasure to bring good luck to other people. The luck he brings (when it is accepted) is nearly always of enormous, life-changing impact, and he usually brings it suddenly. He swoops down on his lucky targets with no advance warning, like some great benevolent bird appearing out of a blue sky that seemed empty a moment before. He thinks often about the circumstances that make him target one man or woman but not another who may be equally deserving. Hidden in those circumstances is the first of the reasons why some are luckier than others.

Bill Battalia is an executive recruiter (or, in business vernacular, "headhunter"). His firm, Battalia, Lotz and Associates, is among the best-known in New York. His clients are major industrial companies, banks, ad agencies, service organizations—most of them large, most of them with well-known names, all of them wealthy. When one of them has an executive-level job to fill and can't fill it by promoting from within, Battalia will be called in. He will be handed some instructions, usually a detailed description of an idealized man or woman whom the company would like to install at the empty desk. "We need a vice-president to untangle our sales problems," he will be told. "This person must be between forty and fifty years old; must have at least ten years' experience in managing sales people, with an excellent track record; must have had on-the-road experience in selling consumer goods to retailers; must speak fluent Spanish as well as English; must be personally attractive, with a flair for speaking before large groups. . . ."

The company, in short, wants to offer a golden chance at self-enlargement to some lucky man or woman yet unknown. The salary and other emoluments being offered are usually more than $35,000 a year and may approach or top $100,000. Battalia knows, obviously, that it will make no sense to seek out people who are already earning the given amount or whose current jobs satisfy them in terms of future prospect. He must conduct the hunt among people for whom the offered job will be a step up—for whom, in general, his sudden appearance out of nowhere will be an important and perhaps colossal stroke of luck.

"There's always a feeling of frustration when we begin a search," he says. "There's always the feeling that hundreds of potential candidates are scattered around the country somewhere, but out of those hundreds we'll only find a fraction. In fact, it's more than a feeling, it's a certainty. Some people just aren't visible."

Battalia conducts his search along many avenues. He

looks at membership lists of professional associations. He goes through trade and professional journals, looking for people who have written articles in the relevant area of expertise. He hangs around business conventions, trade conferences, academic seminars. He also does an enormous amount of telephoning and letter-writing, spreading his question from coast to coast: "Do you know somebody who . . . ?"

The candidates he finds and eventually presents to his client will all be people who, in some way or another, have made themselves visible. Some will have done it deliberately. There are men and women who pay close attention to personal publicity throughout their careers. They join all the associations and societies that will have them, constantly submit articles to professional journals, actively seek speaking engagements, do everything they can think of to keep their names before the world's eyes. Behind this sometimes frantic activity is the consciously held hope that they will be sought out by people bearing bigger and better job offers—by, among others, headhunters like Bill Battalia.

"But of all the people I find," says Battalia, "only a small percentage have waged deliberate publicity campaigns to help me see them. The majority are people who have never given much thought to the possibility of being trapped by a recruiter. A lot of them are simply people who have somehow made themselves *known* to many other people, usually without thinking about it. It's their style. They're gregarious. They go out of their way to be friendly. They talk to strangers. They're joiners, meeters, greeters. If they sit next to somebody on an airplane, they start a conversation. The guy who sells them their morning newspaper is more than just a face. They know his name and how many kids he has and where he went on his vacation. This is the kind of person I can find."

Battalia and his former partner, Jim Lotz, used to spend considerable time analyzing the chains of circumstance that led them to one winning candidate or another. The majority of these turned out to be chains of simple acquaintanceship. A particularly enlightening story concerned Catherine Andrews,* a woman who had started her professional career as a secretary and before age 40, due to the sudden appearance of Battalia and Lotz, became personnel director of a bank. In that one move she more than doubled her salary and vastly broadened her horizons. It seemed like a stroke of blind luck. But analysis of the background seemed to show that, without realizing it, she had made her own luck to a great extent.

What makes her story the more interesting is that there was another life that had paralleled hers for a long time. This other life was lived by a high-school friend, Evelyn Taylor.* Evelyn's life was not lucky. It was an obscure life. The recruiters learned about it only because Catherine Andrews happened to mention it one day at lunch. Catherine said, "I don't know why good luck follows me around like this. Why me? Why not my friend Evelyn?"

The answers to Catherine's questions went back a long way. She and Evelyn Taylor had grown up together in a Detroit suburb. They were inseparable friends in high school, attended a junior college together, went job-hunting together. Job opportunities for women were fairly limited in the late 1950s, and both concluded that their best hope of immediate income was to apply for work as secretaries. An insurance company hired both to work in its billing department.

Within a year the differences between them began to affect their careers. Catherine was by far the friendlier of the two. In the company cafeteria at lunchtime she talked to anybody who turned up near her: people behind her in the food line, people who sat at the same table. The company was large and most employees

* Pseudonym.

were strangers to each other. Catherine liked talking to strangers and finding out about their lives and thoughts. The rich variety of humanity was an entertainment to her, something that relieved the boredom of her job. Evelyn, however, had no interest in strangers unless they were attractive young men. While Catherine talked animatedly with all kinds of people at the cafeteria tables, Evelyn sat next to her, said little, looked bored.

One fellow employee with whom Catherine struck up a casual lunch-hour friendship was an older man who worked in the personnel department. He learned two things about Catherine in their occasional noontime conversations: that she was bored in her present job, and that she had some original ideas about practical ways of broadening women's career opportunities. He passed her in a corridor one day, seemed struck by a sudden idea, and stopped her. There was a job opening in the personnel department, he said. If she was interested he would see what he could do to get her transferred.

It was mainly a secretarial job, but with some interesting features. The company at the time was concerned about the high and increasing turnover rate among its women employees. A decision had been made to interview each departing woman and, if possible, find out what her discontents were and how her job might have been made more attractive. The job opening in the personnel office included the responsibility of conducting these interviews.

Catherine took the job. To Evelyn, still stuck in Accounts Receivable, it seemed like a stroke of pure, blind luck. It did to Catherine too. "The opportunity came to me from a man I hardly knew," she mused many years later. Yes, it was luck. But she had put herself in a position to receive that luck by making herself known to many people. She could not know in advance which of those people would bring a break her way, or when, or what form it would take. But by

129

building a web with many lines, she had increased the statistical chances that something, eventually, would happen.

After two years in that job, Catherine got herself released from what she calls the "secretary trap" and assigned to other duties. She became a full-time interviewer, talking both to outgoing employees and to job applicants. A few years later, through the normal process of attrition from the top and promotion from below, she became assistant personnel director. By both choice and assignment, her main areas of responsibility were the special problems and widening prospects of women employees.

One outgoing employee whom she interviewed, though she found it painful, was Evelyn. Evelyn had found a somewhat better-paying job, but she was still a secretary. No notable good luck had come her way. She has since been married and divorced. Today she is once again working as a secretary.

Catherine came close to marriage twice in the 1960s but in both cases backed out because she foresaw conflicts between her would-be husband and her career. The career continued to be blessed by good luck. Her phone rang one day. A man's voice said, "Ms. Andrews? My name is Bill Battalia . . ."

How and why had Battalia made his way to her? It is an intriguing story.

Battalia's client, a bank, needed a personnel director and was prepared to pay generously to get the right one. The bank had been experiencing some painful, disruptive, and costly difficulties arising from quarrels over sex discrimination among employees. Battalia's instructions were to find an experienced executive who, among other things, commanded a thorough knowledge of women's job rights and had clearly demonstrated a capacity to fulfill women's needs without at the same time upsetting men.

One source of information contacted by Battalia was a woman college professor who had written on such

problems in a labor-relations journal. When Battalia
explained what he wanted, the professor at first sounded
pessimistic. "Most of my contacts are in the academic
world," she said, "people like myself. I may know a
lot about the problems, but as for the actual front-
line experience you're looking for . . ." The professor
paused, then suddenly said, "Wait a minute. It just
happens I was talking to a woman here last week.
We had a seminar on job rights and related problems.
A lot of corporate personnel people attended. This
woman was from some company near Detroit, I think
it was, and she told me about some interesting innova-
tions she's developed up there. Now, if only I can
remember her name. . . ."

Her name, as it turned out, was Catherine Andrews.
She had attended the seminar as part of a continuing
self-education program. True to her own style, she had
talked to everybody in sight. She had accosted the professor one evening when the two of them happened to
be walking across the campus in the same direction.
She had told the professor about her success in halving
employee turnover through a system of informal interviews at lunch, gripe meetings for both sexes, and
other techniques. The professor had been impressed, as
well as charmed and amused by Catherine's eager
friendliness.

It was just one more human contact to Catherine
Andrews—just one of hundreds that she habitually
made each year. She could not foresee that a stunning
piece of luck would come to her through this obscure
college professor. But if it had not been for her habit
of going out of her way to talk to people, the luck
would never have reached her.

If you hope to luck into some pot-of-gold opportunity through a stranger or acquaintance or friend of a
friend, the truth illustrated by Catherine Andrews'
story seems obvious. The bigger your web of friendly
contacts, the better the odds in your favor. You cannot

know what thunderbolt of good fortune is being prepared for you now by some distant engine of fate. You cannot know what complex interconnection of human relationships will guide the thunderbolt in your direction. But you can know, with certainty, that the probability of your getting hit is directly proportional to the number of people who know your name.

It seems obvious. Yet somehow, to many people and probably most, it isn't. It isn't even obvious to some of the lucky ones themselves. Catherine Andrews is typical. Her habit of befriending the motley thousands who drifted through her life wasn't deliberately designed to bring her lucky breaks. She made contact with people for the sake of the contact itself. She simply found people enjoyable. Only in retrospect did she realize that this was the main channel through which some of her luckiest events had flowed.

Kirk Douglas and Charlie Williams, whom you will recall meeting earlier in this book, were similar in this respect. Neither man ever stopped to think about the presence or absence of a spiderweb structure as a reason for good luck or its absence. Douglas' first big break, the one that propelled him from obscurity to the opening of his spectacular career, came through his earlier contact with a then-unknown actress named Lauren Bacall. She was only one of many people whom the gregarious young actor had befriended. By befriending many, he increased the chances that a Lauren Bacall would be among them—somebody whose own good luck might later be translated into good luck for Kirk Douglas. Poor old Charlie Williams, by contrast, was a lifelong loner with very few friendly contacts. The odds that a break would ever come his way through another man or woman were discouragingly small.

Dr. Stephen Barrett of Allentown, Pennsylvania, is a psychiatrist who has done a good deal of thinking about this difference between the lucky and the unlucky. He finds that lucky people as a breed not only have the knack and habit of initiating friendly contacts often. They also have a certain magnetism that makes them the targets of other people's friendly approaches. Dr. Barrett calls this magnetism a "communication field. . . . It seems to say, 'Come and talk to me, we'll get along.'"

Many of Dr. Barrett's patients are high-school girls and college women. For many years, he says, he puzzled over the "dateless-girl phenomenon"—a phenomenon that is familiar in all groups of young people but that few can explain well. The girl who never gets asked out may be as bright and pretty as her more socially active friends—indeed, in some cases may seem to be among the most attractive sexually on the local scene. Her dateless condition may appear on the surface to be a case of random bad luck—the right boy hasn't turned up yet—or may be ascribed to circumstances such as belonging to the wrong clique or having an overstrict mother. But it usually turns out, Dr. Barrett says, that the root of the problem is something in her manner—a communication field—that scares boys, makes them uncomfortable, turns them away. "This same communication field may turn away other girls too. She may be an all-around loner—but the baffling fact, to her, is that she doesn't want to be and can't understand why she is. I've had this kind of girl crying in my office many times."

What is this communication field made of? Dr. Barrett believes there may be hundreds of components: facial expressions, body positions, voice tones, choices of words, ways of using the eyes and holding the head. This cluster of mannerisms is difficult to analyze piece by piece, but the total effect is clearly visible to other people. "We all know instinctively whether somebody likes us or doesn't like us," Dr. Barrett says. "We know whether someone is friendly or unfriendly, warm or cool. We can meet a total stranger and know in seconds whether the stranger does or doesn't want to spend more time with us. In general, people who are considered lucky—people who get lucky breaks handed to them by other people—are those whose communication field is inviting and comfortable."

Despite some recent attempts to analyze "body language" and reduce it to a science, it isn't possible to fake a friendly communication field. No matter how wide your smile or how affectionate your words, people will spot false friendliness quickly. They won't know how they do it, but they will be very sure of their conclusions. This is one of the first lessons that all professional salesmen learn. Tom Watson Sr., founder of IBM and probably one of the most brilliant salesmen who ever walked the earth, used to pound the lesson into young recruits. "If you don't genuinely like your customer," Watson insisted, "the chances are he won't buy." It sounded silly and simplistic to some of the more sophisticated recruits, and some grew tired of hearing it and quit—which was Watson's intention from the beginning. All successful salesmen regard what Watson said as an unarguable truth. If you don't genuinely like strangers, no fakery will hide the fact and you will not go far as a salesman.

One reason why fakery cannot succeed, evidently, is that at least some elements of your communication field aren't under voluntary control. The size of your pupils, for example. Dr. Eckhard Hess, a University of Chicago psychologist, has been studying this peculiar phenomenon for years. He finds that pupil size isn't affected only by the intensity of light, but by whether you like what you are looking at. When you look at something or someone you like, your pupils dilate. When you don't like the view, they contract. Dr. Hess believes this size change is one of the most telling signals that people send to and receive from each other, unconsciously. The eyes, of course, are among our most important instruments of communication. We talk about eyes as warm, shining, steely, cold, and so on. Dr. Hess believes we make these emotional judgments largely on the basis of pupil size. If you talk to some-

body and your pupils are small, you may be judged unfriendly even though you are grinning from ear to ear.

Since you can't walk around all day with pupil-dila-
ting drops in your eyes, and since other elements of
your communication field are undoubtedly just as hard
to fake, what can you do if your field seems to need
adjustment? Dr. Barrett's counsel: "It is easier to
change than you might think. There is certainly no
need to do any faking."

He tells of a 20-year-old college woman who came
to see him, depressed over what seemed to be a condition of chronic datelessness. "She had a beautiful
face," he recalls. "If you had seen her photograph in a
college yearbook you would have said, 'She probably
has more dates than anybody.' But it wasn't so. She
felt lonely. She felt like an outsider, not part of the
crowd."

She and Dr. Barrett talked about her feelings toward
people. These feelings, like everybody's were ex-
tremely complex. Dr. Barrett, honest psychiatrist that
he is, declines to attempt a simplified explanation of
them. But some of the essential facts appeared to be
that she feared rejection, feared being told that she was
disliked or not wanted, and so would not risk making
new contacts unless she absolutely had to. Her fear of
rejection caused that very rejection. Her communication field seemed to say, "Please don't approach me.
I'm afraid of the contact because I'm afraid you won't
like me. It will be less risky for both of us if you stay
away."

Dr. Barrett told her what he holds to be a cardinal
truth about human beings: that we are instinctively dis-
posed to like and help each other. His advice was
mainly that she go out of her way to talk to people, including strangers, and notice how much they wanted to
like and be liked. "I can't catalog all the changes that
went on inside her after that," he says, "but I do know
the change in her communication field was fast." In the

week after her talk with Dr. Barrett, this virtually dateless young woman was asked out four times.

Dr. John Kenneth Woodham, a New Jersey psychologist, is another man who is intrigued by what he calls the "loner syndrome." He agrees with the proposition that lucky breaks often come through other people, and that a loner is therefore unlikely to be lucky. "In any case," he says, "it's no fun to be a loner even if this question of lucky breaks didn't enter the picture. You hear about 'lone wolf' types who are supposedly happy the way they are, but frankly I've never met one. I don't think any human enjoys isolation. That's why I urge isolated people to go out and talk to others, not only people they already know but also strangers. *Especially* strangers. If you're scared of other people or scared of rejection, the quickest cure is to go out and deliberately make contact. Notice what I said: 'cure.' A psychologist doesn't use that word unless he's very, very sure he means it. When you reach out to other people, their response is always delightful. The more you do it, the more you enjoy it."

And the more you enjoy it, presumably, the bigger your pupils grow. If you feel your spiderweb structure is too small, Dr. Woodham's counsel would be that you begin by talking to total strangers, at random, about anything. He points out a peculiar fact: that one of the quickest ways to bring a smile to a stranger's face is to ask for help, even trivial help. Asking for the correct time brings not only a factual reply but usually something extra: "Well, it's about ten past ten. I think that's pretty near right because I checked my watch by the radio this morning. . . ." By adding that extra piece of information, the stranger is saying that he finds it pleasant to talk to you. It delights retailers to be asked for advice about the products they sell. Perhaps the surest conversation-starter on board an airplane is to ask for advice about hotels in the destination city.

Thus does a spiderweb structure begin to grow. The vast majority of those you contact will give you enjoyment and then will drift out of your life, never to be seen or heard of again. But some may be back to bring you good luck.

One of Dr. Woodham's patients was a lonely middle-aged man whose wife had died and whose children had grown and gone. His life was stalled. He seemed to fear it would soon stop. On Dr. Woodham's urging, the man made a deliberate attempt to talk to owner of a stationery store where he customarily bought cigarettes. He had been seeing this woman for years—the store was on a corner where he caught his daily bus to work—but he had never said anything beyond "Good morning," the name of his brand, and "Thanks." He now began by making banal comments about the weather, was encouraged by her friendly response, slowly extended the conversations. In a few weeks they knew each other's names and some trivial details of each other's lives. One detail he volunteered was that his hobby was coin collecting.

He stopped in one morning to find the store owner eagerly waiting for him. She reported that a woman friend of hers, who lived nearby, had a problem. The friend's father had died, leaving her an old house. In a dilapidated bureau in the cellar, apparently overlooked by the estate appraisers, she had found a box of what appeared to be very old European coins. She had no idea of their value or what to do with them. "I remembered you said you were a coin collector," the store owner said. "There are no coin appraisers in town here, and—well, I kind of thought maybe you could. . . ."

The man could and did. The store owner's friend turned out to be an attractive widow his own age and in the same state of loneliness. Today they are married.

Moreover, the European coin collection turned out to be very valuable. Nor is that the end of the story. Luck, when it finally comes, sometimes seems to come in embarrassingly generous bunches. The man didn't want the European collection because his specialty was

The Luck Adjustment

American coins, so his new wife sold them. The couple used the proceeds to go to northern Michigan, a region they both loved, and rent a lakeshore cabin for a month-long honeymoon. While there, the man bought a Michigan lottery ticket and won $25,000.

2.

The Hunching Skill

A HUNCH IS a piece of mind stuff that feels something like knowledge but doesn't feel perfectly trustworthy. Some people trust their hunches more than others do, and of those hunches that are trusted, some turn out to be accurate while others do not. It is obvious that a capacity to generate accurate hunches, and then to trust them and act on them, would go a long way toward producing 'luck." Lucky people as a breed do, indeed, have this capacity to a notable degree.

The hunching skill sounds mysterious, but it turns out not to be. It can be explained in rational terms. Better yet, there is compelling evidence that it can be learned.

Conrad Hilton, the hotel man, owed his monumental success partly to a hunching skill so finely tuned that at times it seemed occult. He steadfastly denied that any paranormal forces were at work in him or around him, but he did sometimes admit to being baffled. "Most of the time I can reconstruct the circumstances of one

139

of these hunches," he once said, "and I can figure out in a general way where it came from. I mean I can explain it—not completely but enough to make it seem less strange. There have been times, though, when I couldn't come up with a good explanation. . . ."

He was trying to buy an old hotel once in Chicago. The owner was selling on the basis of sealed bids. All the bids were to be opened on a certain date, and the hotel would go to the highest bidder. Several days before the deadline, Hilton submitted a bid of $165,000. He went to bed that night feeling vaguely disturbed. The next morning he awoke with a strong hunch that his bid was not going to win. "It just didn't feel right," he said later, helplessly, when asked to explain. Acting on this strange intuition, he submitted another bid: $180,000.

It was the highest bid. The next one down was $179,800.

Dolores N., a Philadelphia bank teller, is in her late twenties and single. She considers this a fortunate state. She almost married two years ago, and she talks about that near miss the way someone else might talk about a hair's-breadth escape from some ghastly accident. "If I had married," she says, "it would have been a disaster. He married another woman after I turned him down, and today he is in jail and she is in debt, trying to take care of a baby, drinking too much—in absolutely awful shape. There but for the grace of God . . ."

Some men and women seem consistently unlucky in love. Dolores N. considers herself consistently lucky, and she attributes this to a hunching skill. "Some call it woman's intuition," she says, "but that's stupid. There are men who have intuition, and there are women who haven't. Like with this man I almost married. My sister liked him, and so did my mother. So did the poor woman who finally married him. But with me, there was this sudden feeling from nowhere. . . ."

The man, Ted, was soft-spoken and charming. Dolores met him at a party given by one of her co-workers at the bank. He told her he worked for a public-relations agency. After a very quick courtship he asked her to marry him, and she said yes.

They were together nearly every night after work, usually meeting at restaurants near his office or hers. "Until about a week before the wedding I was madly in love with him," Dolores recalls. "But then, one night, this hunch hit me. I still don't know how or why. It was a night like any other night. We talked about the things lovers talk about—you know, some silly things and some important things, like our plans for the future. We had a couple of glasses of wine, and then he went to the men's room. And while I was sitting there at the table by myself, this funny little thought came to me: *Something isn't right. Something isn't true.*"

The logical part of her mind, the part that demanded tangible facts to work with, scorned the hunch and ordered it to go away. But it was back the next day. On impulse, during her midmorning coffee break, she went to a telephone and called Ted at his office. A woman on the phone said, "I'm sorry, he is no longer with us."

Dolores still could not marshal any specific facts to support her hunch, but it was now stronger and more detailed than before. It said, "Ted is a man in some kind of chronic financial difficulty. If I marry him, I marry trouble."

She called off the wedding. There was an angry scene, of course. It was made all the more painful to her by the fact that she could not offer Ted any rational explanation of her wish to end the relationship. But she trusted her hunch and stuck with it. Ted vanished from her life.

She had met a few of his friends and acquaintances during the courtship, and over the next year she tried to find out who and what Ted really was. It turned out that he was a compulsive gambler. He was deeply in debt to his family, friends, banks, and loan sharks. He had been fired from his public-relations job for nonperformance. He would tell people in the office that he was going out to visit a client and then would spend the day at the racetrack. Two years after Dolores turned him away, he was convicted of check forgery and sent to jail.

C. C. Hazard* is a retired stockbroker. He is comfortably rich. When people ask him how they, too, can beat the stock market, he refers them to his book, *Confessions of a Wall Street Insider*. The book, like Hazard himself, is prickly and argumentative and was not well received on the Street when it was published a few years ago. One of its major themes is that ordinary small-time plungers—you and I, that is—cannot gain much by subscribing to advisory services, studying market statistics, drawing charts, listening to economic forecasts from Washington, or applying logic in any other fashion. Hazard holds that the market is an engine of emotion rather than reason, and therefore its movements cannot be predicted by rational means.

How can they be predicted? Sometimes, says Hazard, by hunching. "It took me a long time to learn to trust my hunches," he once told me. "When I first hit the Street in the 1950s I did all that rational stuff—studied the GNP and all that—but I was no righter than if I'd guided myself by tossing a coin. Time and again I'd find myself going against a hunch and ending up sorry. All the big pundits would be saying the market was going up, and they'd have all kinds of neat logical reasons for saying it, and I'd bet with them even though I had a hunch they were wrong. They would turn out wrong—not always, but enough times to make me start wondering. I finally told myself, 'What the hell, if these rational techniques are no better than tossing a coin, hunches couldn't be any worse.' I began

* Pseudonym.

listening to my own hunches, and today I'm glad I did."

Hazard had a grand hunch late in 1968. He isn't sure when it first started to nag him, but he does remember that he first articulated it to himself one Friday night at Oscar's Delmonico, a historic watering spot not far from the New York Stock Exchange. It had been a buoyant, high-volume week on the exchanges, and the bar at Oscar's was crowded with brokers, specialists, fund operators, freelance speculators, and others, some of them drunk, most of them happy, all of them talking loudly.

"I had a couple of drinks with two friends," Hazard recalls, "and they went off somewhere and left me by myself. My wife was out on the West Coast that week visiting her family. I didn't feel like going home, so I stayed at the bar for another drink. I'm standing there in the crowd thinking my own thoughts when suddenly this little guy next to me, a guy I've never seen before or since, turns to me and says, 'Christ, what a market it's been, huh?' He's grinning from ear to ear, this little guy, he looks happy enough to climb up on the bar and dance a jig. Well, I should be happy too. I've made so much money in the sixties that it's immoral, and sixty-eight looks like the best year yet. But I can't get into the little guy's mood. And somehow—get this, it's crazy—somehow, instead of cheering me up as he jabbers in my ear, the guy *scares* me."

Hazard has not since been able to pinpoint the source of his sudden fear. He thinks there may have been a submerged hysterical quality in the little man's face or voice or gestures. "Whatever it was, it kind of reinforced the feeling that had been needling me for weeks. When I looked around the bar at all those other guys and listened to them talk, I felt this same scary thing in the air. The only way I can describe this feeling is, it reminded me of when my kids were young and we used to build towers out of colored wood blocks. We made a contest out of it. We'd take turns

143

building the tower up, one block at a time. The tower would get taller and wobblier. Whoever put the last block on and made it fall, lost. The feeling I had at Oscar's was like that feeling of working on a tall tower. The taller it gets, the more fun it is and the happier everybody gets—but the scarier it gets, too. You know the tower is going to collapse pretty soon. That was what my hunch felt like in sixty-eight. I had this feeling there were terrible times ahead. There was this nervous quality in the air."

Few rational analysts were making any such forecasts as 1968 ended. Hazard, however, sold virtually all his stocks. The market began to fall soon afterward. By mid-1970 most of Hazard's stocks were worth less than half of what he had sold them for. Some haven't recovered to this day.

Where does an accurate hunch come from? Many psychologists and other authorities think they can explain it without resorting to ESP or the occult. In essence, the theory is this:

A hunch is a conclusion that is based on perfectly real data—on objective facts that have been accurately observed, efficiently stored, logically processed in your mind. The facts on which the hunch is based, however, are *facts you don't consciously know*. They are stored and processed on some level of awareness just below or behind the conscious level. This is why a hunch comes with that peculiar feeling of almost-but-not-quite-knowing. It is something that you think you know, but you don't know how you know it.

Among the most articulate on this intriguing subject is a New York psychologist, Dr. Eugene Gendlin. A lean, dark-haired man of Russian descent, Dr. Gendlin has spent most of his professional life studying this not-quite-conscious level of awareness. He has built a whole new therapeutic approach around the study. If he will permit me to give an oversimplified description of his work for the sake of brevity, it might be said that he teaches his patients, in effect, to "hunch" their way through their problems. He has developed techniques for deliberately probing down into that deep-lying storage bin of buried data, the place where hunches come from. He says anybody can learn to do this. As a matter of fact, in a book that he has written on his approach, he makes the startling assertion that therapists such as himself aren't necessary at all, except perhaps for the most severely disturbed people. Once you learn to "focus"—his term for the probing process—you become your own therapist forever after.

One definition of "luck" would certainly be this: Luck is being somebody whose emotional troubles never get bad enough to require professional help. Luck is having a serene life, with occasional bright splashes of joy. Dr. Gendlin believes lucky people, in this sense, are often people who have discovered intuitively how to plumb that well of subsurface knowledge inside themselves. He isn't interested particularly in people who have hunches about the stock market, but in people who have the generalized ability to "feel" their way through life and its problems and who consistently choose the best route for themselves. His "focusing" technique is designed to produce serenity, not money. For purposes of our study of luck, however, there is no need to make such a distinction. A hunch is a hunch. If you could learn to hunch effectively, presumably you could use the skill for any purpose that is important to you personally.

Dr. Gendlin, in explaining his approach, begins by pointing out that you take in vastly more data every day than can possibly be stored in your conscious mind. For example, think of any man or woman who has played a prominent role in your life. There are thousands of data bits, probably millions, that describe this person as perceived by you—so many bits that it would take you years to list them even if you could retrieve them all from memory. They would include data about the physical appearance, the voice, the gestures and mannerisms, the attitudes, ways of thinking, emotional responses, preferences in work, play, food, clothes, cars. They would include data about interactions between this person and you: all the times when you were happy together, angry, bored, worried, scared. The list would be literally endless because new data would come in with each new day when the two of you made contact. Despite the huge length of this list, however, it is stored somewhere inside you and is instantly retrievable. If you glance away from this page now and conjure up a vision of this man or woman, he or she will come instantly into your mind—will come *whole*. All the data will somehow be there: everything that means "Joe" or "Mary" to you.

Where did the data come from? Obviously not from your conscious mind itself—not from the logical, thinking brain that processes data bits one by one. If you meet this friend on the street, you recognize him or her instantly—and, moreover, you instantly feel an emotional response that is appropriate to the person and to all past and present circumstances. This swift process of recognition and reaction takes place with no intellectual figuring out on your part. Too many bits of data are involved for conscious ratiocination. The process bypasses your reasoning mind almost entirely.

The example shows that it is perfectly possible to know something without being quite able to explain how—without being able to list all the discrete data bits that support the feeling of knowing. Suppose I ask you what clues you use to recognize your friend on the street. Do you analyze the shape of the nose? The manner of walking? The mole on the cheek? The rumpled clothes? You would have to answer that all these clues and uncounted others mix to form the instantaneous impression. You don't truly know what clues you use or how you put them together. Yet if I were to suggest that you might therefore be mistaken in identifying this person—that your factual evidence is too shaky to be reliable—you would laugh. When you meet your friend, there is no doubt in your mind about whom you have met. Without knowing how, you *know*.

Another example. Your friend telephones you. No name need be spoken. You need only hear a few words, and you recognize the voice. How? If you tried to describe that voice to me so that I, too, could recognize it, you would find the task impossible. As a matter of fact the New York Telephone Company once tried to find how people recognize each others' voices on the phone and gave up in despair. It turned out that the recognition process doesn't depend on consciously known data. Yet despite this lack of discrete data, no doubts assail you when you hear a familiar voice on the phone. You *know* who it is.

In effect, this kind of knowing is a species of hunch. You know, but you don't know how you know.

A hunch is built of data that you can't quite pull up to the conscious level—facts that you can't list, can't identify, can't exhibit to prove the reliability of your conclusion to anybody else (or indeed to yourself). Yet if the hunch is a good one, the facts do exist. They are stored inside you somewhere. True, it is frustrating not to be able to get at them and inspect them. But the mere fact that they aren't available need not nullify the power and usefulness of the hunch. You can drive a car without necessarily knowing how the engine is put together.

Seen in this way—as derived from objective data not consciously known—a hunch becomes less mysterious. Conrad Hilton's hunch about that hotel bid, for instance, could have welled up from great stores of facts in the recesses of his mind. He had been in the hotel business throughout his adult life. Ever since he bought his first hotel as a young man in Texas, he had been gathering knowledge about the business: millions of facts, many more than his conscious mind could juggle all at once. Moreover, in bidding on that Chicago hotel, he undoubtedly knew much about the sellers and about the competing bidders—knew it, again, without being able to articulate it in the form of specific facts. When his rational brain assembled some facts and based a bid on them, the other part of his mind rummaged in a huge dark warehouse of other facts and concluded that the bid was too low. He trusted the hunch, and it was magnificently right.

Dolores N.'s hunch about Ted must have arisen in a similar way. The hunch may have been based on observed details that her thinking brain considered trivial: some things Ted said, perhaps, or certain mannerisms, or a shifting of the eyes in response to certain questions or overtures by her. These details, dismissed as unimportant, were forgotten—but not forgotten. They sank from conscious awareness to another level. Down there, they were processed and examined and put together with other facts. The result was a hunch that whispered, "Something isn't true."

As for C. C. Hazard, like all good salesmen he is a gregarious soul who spends his days talking to people, listening to them, observing them. He makes contact with scores of people in an average day, thousands a year. His conscious mind doesn't retain all the personal impressions that he takes in, but the other part of his mind does. It stores them, sorts them, adds them gradually into a single cumulative impression. And finally, as in 1968, it produces a seemingly mysterious hunch: " . . . a nervous quality in the air . . . terrible times ahead. . . ."

This not-quite-conscious way of processing data used to be thought mainly feminine and was called "woman's intuition." A few years ago *Vogue* magazine rounded up some psychiatrists and others for a symposium on this elusive subject. Their consensus was that the hunching talent is not innately stronger in either sex, but that, until recently, it was stronger in women because of the way society was built. Men prided themselves on what they considered their superior reasonableness. As a corollary, they suppressed feelings. The emotional, the mystical, the vague: these were felt to be feminine or, at best, not powerfully masculine. Women, most of whom had small chance to use their thinking brains in the old societies (and were often ridiculed when they did), felt the need to show they were superior to men in other ways. One such way was "woman's intuition."

She: "Joe and Jane are having an affair."

He: "How do you know?"

She: "I just know."

He: "That's dumb. You don't have any facts. . . ."

Thus did each sex jockey for position by expressing what were felt to be its special qualities. The man demanded objective facts because that was a fine masculine attitude. The woman, by demonstrating her hunching skill, preserved her "mystery" and her measure of power over the man. Both sexes agreed that intuition was feminine because both profited from the notion. Some remnants of this sex distinction are still alive today, but it seems unlikely that they will last long.

The difference between the sexes was that many women encouraged this process within themselves and were comfortable with it, while many men didn't and weren't. However, some impressively bright men dismissed the male tradition and freely admitted that intuition was an important part of their survival equipment. Conrad Hilton was an example. So was Alfred P. Sloan, perhaps the most brilliant of General Motors' presidents. Sloan was asked once how he could possibly marshal all the facts needed to make sensible decisions on major questions such as where to locate a new plant, how many cars to build, how much to spend on advertising. Sloan replied frankly that he couldn't hope to put all the relevant facts together and didn't even try. "The final act of business judgment," he said, "is intuitive."

Sloan's words apply equally well to most of the judgments we make in daily living. Whether we like

149

it or not, life requires us to hunch our way constantly through big decisions and small. Should I take this job? Is this realtor telling me the truth when he says the cellar doesn't leak? Will this woman be angry if I . . . ? Seldom do we have quite enough facts. Seldom can we make exclusively rational deductions and decisions. Unlike Sherlock Holmes, who could always supply a magnificently logical explanation for each of his conclusions, we ordinary thinkers more often find ourselves making choices that we can't quite explain. "I bought the house because—well, because it felt right." Lucky people, as a group, often turn out to be people whose hunches at life's major and minor crossroads are trustworthy. They are people who never buy houses with leaky cellars. They never drive out of used-car lots with lemons. They never buy stocks just before bear markets begin. They never get stuck in the slowest lines at airport ticket counters. Their domestic, social, sexual, and economic lives are serene.

If you want good luck, the hunching talent is a useful if not essential piece of equipment. How can you develop it? There are three major rules to follow.

The First Rule: Learn to Assess the Data Base

A hunch comes unbidden: a strong feeling that such-and-such is true. How do you know whether to trust it?

The first part of the answer, in C. C. Hazard's words: "I ask myself how solid the underlying data base might be. Obviously I don't know what facts this hunch is based on and have no hope of knowing them. But what I *can* do is ask whether these facts might exist. I ask: Is it conceivable that I've gathered a pool of data on this situation without realizing it? Have I been in a position to gather these facts? Even though I can't see them, is it reasonable to think they are there? If the answer is yes and if the hunch feels strong, I tend to go with it."

In this book we have talked to people who had hunches about lotteries and slot machines, and won. To Hazard, the fact that they won is irrelevant. He would never trust that kind of hunch. There is no possibility that such a hunch can well up from some hidden pool of facts inside you. There *are* no facts about the results of future lottery drawings or about the random meshing of cogs at some future moment inside a slot machine. Any such hunch, therefore, should be dismissed as untrustworthy.

Or, to draw an example from Hazard's own beloved Wall Street, consider the peculiar story of Jesse Livermore. Livermore was a famous speculator who flourished on the Street earlier in this century. He was known for uncannily accurate hunches that he himself couldn't explain and never tried to. His most talked-about hunch hit him one spring day in 1906. Without knowing why, he suddenly became convinced that the price of Union Pacific stock was about to drop. Accordingly he walked into a broker's office and sold thousands of shares short. (For those not familiar with Street jargon, suffice it to say that short selling is a risky maneuver in which you can make immodest amounts of money when the stock price falls—but can bankrupt yourself rapidly if it rises.)

According to contemporary accounts, Livermore seemed puzzled by his own action that day. Well he might have been. A bull market was in progress, and Union Pacific was one of the hottest stocks on the board. There was no good reason to sell it short. Yet the next day, still looking vaguely puzzled, he returned to the brokerage and sold more thousands of shares short.

The day after that, April 18, San Francisco was struck by a catastrophic earthquake. Huge amounts of Union Pacific equipment and potential earnings were buried beneath the rubble. The stock price dropped like a stone, and Jesse Livermore walked away richer by about $300,000.

Hindsight tells us that his hunch was correct—but that doesn't mean he was smart to bet his money on it. No facts about the impending earthquake could have been available to him in advance. The hunch had no data base. To risk bankruptcy over it was probably foolish.

As a matter of fact, Livermore did bankrupt himself more than once in his eventful life. His hunches were not always good, particularly toward the end. He lost heavily in the late 1930s. One afternoon just before Christmas, 1940, perhaps brooding about departed luck, he walked into a New York hotel, had a couple of drinks, went to the men's room, and shot himself.

In the last analysis, his hunches must be counted untrustworthy—even those that were right. They were untrustworthy, that is, in terms of the kind of hunch we have been discussing here: the kind that is presumed to be based on objective fact and logical processing. This type of hunch might be labeled "rational." If you believe in or suspect the existence of psychic or occult forces, of course, you would say that rational hunches aren't the only possible kind. The other kind—Jesse Livermore's kind—might be labeled "paranormal." Anyone who trusts the paranormal would point to Livermore's superb Union Pacific hunch and insist that there was something behind it—not objective facts, but something else. Unarguably, that hunch was stunningly correct.

It is beyond the scope of this book to make a case either for or against the paranormal. If you believe in such forces they may help you, and if you don't they probably won't. But everybody can make use of rational hunching. We will come back to the paranormal in a while. For the moment let's go on with our study of rational hunches and the problem of assessing the data base.

"A hunch is only as good as the sum of past experience that produces it," says Dr. Natalie Shainess, a New York psychiatrist who has studied the differences between people who do and don't consider themselves lucky. "You can trust a hunch only if you've had experience in the situation it deals with. I often do intuitive things in treating patients, for instance. I have hunches about what will and won't work. I trust these hunches because I've had long experience in this field. I take them to be true perceptions on a nonconscious level. But if I had a hunch about some field I didn't know—let's say a hunch about making a killing in soybean futures—I wouldn't trust it. It couldn't be a true perception."

When a hunch comes, always ask yourself whether the underlying facts could be there. Ask whether you *could* have absorbed data about the situation. This is the First Rule of hunching. Under it we can list these corollary rules:

Corollary 1. Never trust a hunch about somebody you have just met.

Unlucky people tend to make commitments on the basis of first impressions. Lucky people go back for a second look.

If you met somebody half an hour ago and have already developed a hunch about his or her honesty, goodwill, intelligence, or other character traits, dismiss the hunch as unreliable. You probably have not had time to absorb enough data. Love at first sight is fun but very, very chancy. Second sight and third sight are better. Hindsight, when it tells a story not told by first sight, can be painful.

Never commit either your emotions or your money on the basis of a first-sight hunch. Let's suppose you are shopping for a new car. Several makes and models attract you. Your main concern is over the quality and willingness of the servicing. When things go wrong with your new car, how well will you be treated? One dealer impresses you as particularly frank, honest, willing to work hard to please you. Should you trust this hunch?

Absolutely not. If the man is a good salesman, he is a good actor. He knows how to make an appealing first impression. Ask yourself what facts your hunch could be based on. Perhaps it is based only on an irrelevant memory. Perhaps the man's face reminds you of someone you knew and liked years ago.

Put your checkbook away for a day or so. Go back and talk to the man at least one more time. Drop in when he isn't expecting you. Absorb the "feel" of his shop. Listen when he is talking to others. None of this will guarantee that you are buying your car at the right place, but it will vastly improve your chances of making a good choice. On second or third sight you may feel little tendrils of worry creeping in around the edges of your hunch. If that happens, you may elect to take your business elsewhere.

Corollary 2. Never fall back on hunching to avoid work.

First find out all you can about the situation in which you need to make a decision. Steep yourself in it. Hungrily seek the facts of it. Try to reach your decision first on the basis of consciously known data. If you can't, then fall back on hunching—but only then.

Remember Alfred P. Sloan's remark: "The final act of business judgment. . . ." That word "final" is important. If that final act is to produce useful results, some acts of hard work must precede it.

The wish to avoid work—which may spring from many diverse roots, including plain laziness—produces very bad hunches. They are hunches without factual substance. In fact they are not true hunches at all. They are only daydreams.

One man who emphasizes this point is a University of California psychiatrist, Dr. William Boyd, who used to teach a course entitled "Gambling, Risk-Taking, and Speculative Investment." Dr. Boyd is fascinated by the phenomenon of hunching. He has studied it, particularly among compulsive gamblers, who almost always use the hunching talent badly—and, of course, almost always lose.

There are many theories about the emotional torments of compulsive gamblers and the "accident-prone" and other chronically unlucky people. One widely held theory—you can hear it glibly repeated at any cocktail party if you bring up the subject—is that such people harbor a subconscious wish to punish or destroy themselves and so go out of their way to set up situations in which they will lose. This self-punishing urge may exist in a few people, but the evidence to support the theory is slim. In all my wanderings in search of luck stories and luck theories, I have never personally met a man or woman who wanted to lose. Dr. Boyd's findings seem much easier to swallow. Says he: "Compulsive gamblers are usually people who, among other things, simply don't like to work. Many worked and tried hard in some past period of their lives but were badly rewarded. They felt like 'suckers.' Their worst fear is to feel that way again, so they're reluctant to put out any effort. They want something for nothing. They depend on what they call 'hunches'— vague premonitions which, of course, usually turn out to be wrong."

Dr. Boyd says he once had a patient who, for a while, studied and successfully used the "Thorp System" of counting cards at blackjack. This system, invented by a University of California mathematician, Professor Edward O. Thorp, works so well that casinos quite rudely discourage its use and will even eject a "counter" when they recognize one. However, to master the system requires work—hard work, hours and hours of it. "My patient finally abandoned it," says Dr. Boyd. "He frankly admitted it was too much work for him. He went back to his old system of relying on 'hunches' and losing."

Any time you want to act on what you fondly think

is a hunch, ask yourself earnestly whether you are merely inventing an excuse for avoiding honest study—or for avoiding people who might answer your questions. False hunching of this kind has generated unmeasured gallons of tears in and around Wall Street, for example. You can hope for Jesse Livermore's kind of luck (or pre-cognition, or whatever it was), but unless you are a devotee of the psychic or occult, to count on it could be foolish. Unsuccessful speculators do count on it often. They tell themselves, "I have a hunch this stock will go up," and they buy without doing any real homework. This helps explain why they are unsuccessful. A hunch without a solid data base is not a rational hunch.

An excellent description of successful hunching is given by financial editor Chris Welles in his 1975 book, *The Last Days of the Club*. Welles is talking about Fred Mates, a spectacularly successful mutual-fund manager in the go-go years of the 1960s. An associate of Mates told Welles: "Fred will watch a company for a long time, gathering information from technical and trade magazines . . . and many other places. Then all of a sudden one more piece of information will come and Fred will announce that at last the company 'smells right,' as he puts it. When he tries to tell you why, you can follow him about 90 percent of the way but then he leaves you. That last 10 percent is too subjective. It's the area where artists work."

It is the area where hunches are made. Mates could not explain how his hunches were formed, any more than any other huncher can. But he knew that you cannot rely on a hunch unless it stands on a solid basis of homework.

Like other go-go funds, the Mates Fund ran out of luck when the great bull market died in 1969. Mates eventually left Wall Street to open a singles' bar, explaining to Welles that "people want to drink to forget the stock market." It is hard to say why that brilliant hunching talent went awry. Perhaps one reason was that Mates violated the Second Rule.

The Second Rule: Never Confuse a Hunch with a Hope

If a hunch tells you something is true, and if you badly want it to be true, regard the hunch with suspicion.

"A lot of bad hunches are just strong wishes in disguise," says Dr. Natalie Shainess. This is a second reason why she would reject her hypothetical hunch about "making a killing in soybean futures." When hunches and hopes are churning about in the mind and gut, they feel confusingly alike.

Dr. Boyd reports that this confusion is a major problem of unsuccessful speculators and gamblers. "When you want something a great deal," he says, "it is very easy to talk yourself into believing it will happen. A gambler will tell me, 'I've got a hunch I'll clean up at the track next week.' I ask why he thinks so. He says, 'Well, I've been losing so long that my luck's got to turn. I can feel it coming.' There's no sense arguing with the man. The wish is the mother of the hunch. He goes out to the track, bets the long shots and loses everything he has."

It is never possible to be perfectly sure about a hunch, of course. The very nature of a hunch is that it is formed from unknown facts, correlated in unknown ways. But it is possible to examine the hunch, feel around the edges of it, test its strength and composition. One executive of a major fast-food chain has a method of doing this: he deliberately tries to make his hunch break down.

"I argue with it," he says. "I tell myself, 'Listen, you only want to give this guy a franchise because you're sorry about his kid's illness. He's a weakling. In a rich market he'd do well, but if a big competitor moved in up the street he'd just sit around feeling sorry for himself. Also, he's sloppy. He'd let his franchise get so crummy that the family trade would shun it. He'd let it degenerate into a teen hangout. . . .' I actually try to imagine the man doing all these things wrong. I set up scenes in my mind—greasy tabletops, the help insulting the customers, and so on. I kind of ask myself, 'Is any of this possible?' And then I wait around for a few days and see what my hunch tells me. Usually it says, 'No, not possible.' But a few times I've heard it say, 'Yes, it could happen.' The original good feeling I had about this man or woman begins to seem less good. Then I have to reassess everything, and maybe I'll end by turning the person down."

You may not find it necessary or useful to go through any such process of deliberately attacking your own hunch. The most important step of all is the first: recognizing that you are in a situation where hunch and hope may become confused. When that awareness hits you, it will make you careful.

The Third Rule: Make Room for Hunches to Grow

Hunches are made of facts, but they come as feelings. According to Dr. Eugene Gendlin, "Many people or most are not really in touch with their own feelings." This undoubtedly is a reason why many men and women, perhaps the majority, lack a well-developed hunching talent. To hunch soundly you must listen to your feelings, respect them, give them a full hearing. This rule is probably the most crucial of the three.

Corollary 1. Don't smother a hunch by "figuring out."

This is the key lesson that Dr. Gendlin pounds into

his patients. The patient's problem is to get at the roots of some personal difficulty and sense what direction to take through it. Dr. Gendlin tells the patient to sit quietly, relax, and as far as possible suspend all intellectual processes. "Don't try to analyze anything," he urges. "Don't intellectualize. Don't *figure out*. Don't say, 'It must be . . .' Don't say, 'X is true, therefore Y must also be true.' Just ask yourself what you *feel* about this situation. Let the feeling float up freely."

A feeling about a situation, says Dr. Gendlin, always contains vastly more than could have been figured out intellectually. The feeling is the stored total of the situation as the mind and body have been experiencing it. It is an enormously rich mass of facts and impressions, many of them without words to label them. If you insist always on approaching problems and decisions in a strictly analytical way, dealing only with those parts that can be tidily described in words and related to consciously known facts, you are imposing very great restrictions on yourself. That is like going out to prospect for oil with a drill that will go only three feet deep. Most of the riches lie deeper.

Lucky people, as a breed, know instinctively how to probe down to the depths where hunch stuff lies buried. Dr. Gendlin's cheery message is that anybody can learn this skill. He teaches his patients to make contact with a large, vague, generalized feeling and then "focus" on ever smaller parts of it. As he has explained the process in several professional journals and in his book, *Focusing*, it works something like this:

You ask yourself: "What do I feel about this situation?"

The feeling replies (perhaps not in words): "Scared, worried."

You ask the feeling to define itself more narrowly: "Scared in what way?"

The possibly wordless reply: "It's a feeling of things getting out of control . . . like I'm trying to hold something up but it's starting to collapse around me."

The Luck Adjustment

"Where's the worst part of this collapse?"

"It's something about George. I have a hunch he's working against me when I'm not around."

"Working against me how? Doing what?"

And so on. You don't ask for reasons or explanations, just for more and more of the feeling. People who are instinctive hunchers go through some such process at every decision-making point of their lives. It is likely that children often make decisions and discern truths by hunching. As they grow older, some retain the skill but others smother it with analytical reasoning, perhaps because that seems more sensible and adult. In fact the smothering is often encouraged by parents.

Child: "Susan doesn't like me."

Parent: "How do you know?"

Child: "I just know."

Parent: "But what does she do? Spit at you? Kick you?"

Child: "No, nothing like that. She acts friendly, and all. It's just—oh, I don't know."

Parent: "But that's stupid You don't have any *reason*. . . ."

Thus do some of us lose an inborn talent. We become embarrassed to use it. We lose the willingness to trust it.

Corollary 2. Collect "soft" facts along with hard.

Soft facts are feelings, impressions—or, to use a fad word of the 1960s, "vibrations." Hard facts—the overt, the objective—seem more real to many people. Many, as a result, restrict themselves to observing hard facts alone and dismiss all other observations as irrelevant, trival, or unreliable. If you habitually restrict yourself this way, your hunching talent doesn't get any exercise.

A man and a woman go to a party. A friend later asks them what the party was like.

The man reports: "Well, George and Evelyn were

there, and Ed and Fay, and . . . we had barbecued spareribs. . . ."

The woman reports: "It was fun to see a lot of those old friends again, but there was some kind of stiffness in the air. I had this feeling we were all competing with each other. You know, showing off about how far we'd come since the old days, and how smart our kids had grown. . . ."

The man has restricted himself to hard facts. The woman is dealing with soft facts—hunch stuff. If somebody challenges them to produce evidence that their observations are accurate, the man will, of course, have the more provable case by far. The woman may not be able to produce any proof at all. It takes courage to collect soft facts that can't be backed with objective proof—and that may be a reason why the man has avoided doing so. Yet if this man and woman are later called on to make a difficult decision involving somebody at that party, it is likely that the woman's hunch will be the more reliable.

"The ability to perceive vibrations improves with practice," says New York psychiatrist Dr. Abraham Weinberg. Many of Dr. Weinberg's patients are Wall Street brokers and speculators. He has spent much of his life trying to find why some of them consistently make more correct guesses about the stock market than do others, and he concludes that the more successful ones are those who, among other things, consistently collect impressions as well as hard facts. "To become good at it, you have to do it every day, in every situation," he says. "Keep forcing yourself to perceive more than you see. Keep asking yourself, 'What are the vibrations here, what do I feel?' A lot of people scorn this approach because vibrations don't seem to come through the five ordinary senses. They seem occult, mystical. But vibrations—or call them impressions if you like, drifting impressions—are quite real. To make use of them, you must make yourself fully receptive to them."

Dr. Weinberg suspects that these "vibrations" may sometimes be partly telepathic in nature. As we have seen, so do many other researchers. But he admits that it isn't really necessary to explain them in terms of ESP. They can be explained as everyday hunch stuff: observed facts that have been collected on some other-than-conscious level.

My personal preference is to explain them without ESP—which is why I prefer to call them "soft facts" instead of "vibrations." If the idea of ESP appeals to you, that makes no difference at all. No matter what explanation you favor, the world of feelings and impressions plainly exists. It is a world full of riches for those who take the trouble to use it.

3.

"Audentes Fortuna Juvat"

"FORTUNE FAVORS THE bold," says the old Latin aphorism. At first glance this seems like windy nonsense. One imagines it was authored by some Roman general trying to tune up an unenthusiastic bunch of troops for the next day's battle. It sounds like empty optimism, a bundle of brave-sounding words without any substantial foundation. For it is obvious that Mother Fortune, though she may be good to the bold sometimes, clobbers them at other times. A conflicting motto might be held equally true: "Take no chances and you won't get hurt"—or, as we used to say in the army, "Never volunteer for anything."

Yet here is an odd fact. As a group, lucky people tend to be bold people. The most timid men and women I've met in my travels have also been, with exceptions, the least lucky.

Why is this? It could be pointed out first that luck probably creates boldness. If life hasn't hurt you a great deal, you are probably somewhat more willing to

163

take chances than somebody whom fortune has often kicked in the face.

But it also works the other way around. Boldness helps create good luck. The old Latin aphorism is not unequivocally true, but it turns out to have some very important elements of truth in it. Let's examine it and see what it is made of. *Audentes fortuna juvat.*

The class of 1949 from Princeton University celebrated its 25th graduation anniversary in 1974. The Forty-niners, as they call themselves, have always been a fairly cohesive and introspective group, fond of polling themselves periodically to see what the members have been doing and thinking. Their twenty-fifth anniversary was the occasion for an unusually complicated, detailed poll, and it revealed something about luck.

Life and luck had of course produced much happiness and much sadness for the Forty-niners in the eventful quarter-century since they first challenged the world as independent adults. In June, 1949, the graduating class consisted of about 770 hopeful young men. By the time of the twenty-fifth reunion, about 25 of those men were dead—killed in war, in accidents, by disease: victims of luck's ultimate and irrevocable caprice. Another 40 or so were "lost," as the Alumni Bureau sadly put it—meaning that nobody knew where they were or what had happened to them. Of the remaining 700, about one-third filled out the anonymous twenty-fifth-year questionnaire.

One question was perhaps harder to answer than all the rest put together. It asked each man to travel backward in time and become, once again, the young blood he had been on Commencement Day, 1949.

It is a bright June day, filled with dreams and mysteries. The young man steps up onto the platform to receive his diploma. The university president shakes his hand, gives him his sheepskin, and then gravely offers him something else, a special gift. The young man may refuse the gift if he wishes. It is a crystal ball of guaranteed accuracy. In it, if he accepts it, he will see the man he is to become a quarter-century hence, in 1974. The crystal ball will reveal everything of importance about the future man: the professional and financial accomplishments, the marital and sexual satisfactions, the family and social relationships, the state of health, the whole galaxy of human pleasures and pains.

The young man accepts the gift. He gazes into it and sees himself in the mid-1970s. The question is. What is his reaction? Is he pleasantly surprised? Or is the future man just about what he had expected? Or is he unimpressed or disappointed?

Some two-fifths of the respondents thought the young man would have reacted with surprise and pleasure. Another two-fifths felt he would have been contented but not surprised: the 25-year outcome was in general what he had planned or predicted. The remaining fifth felt he would have been unimpressed or disappointed.

The top two-fifths—the pleased-surprised group—might be called the lucky ones. These were obviously men who had been in the right places at the right times. Life had treated them better than they had once thought they could count on. By contrast, the unimpressed-disappointed fifth had not been treated as well as they had expected or hoped. Perhaps in some cases this was because their expectations had been set too high in 1949. But as a general rule, this lower fifth might be called unlucky. For various reasons, fewer pleasant events had happened to these men than to the others.

For what reasons? Probably the lack of a good spiderweb structure contributed to these disappointing results in many cases, and the lack of a sound hunching talent in others. The poll offered no way to make reliable judgments about these factors. But it did

165

seem to show something else quite clearly. The unlucky fifth lacked boldness.

This conclusion arose from a remarkable correlation with another question in the Forty-niners' poll. The question asked each man how many different companies he had worked for (if employed) or how many separate ventures he had launched (if self-employed) since graduation. It turned out that the men who answered this question with the biggest numbers were, on the whole, the most likely to consider themselves lucky. Of all the men who had moved boldly in their lives—had held six or more jobs since graduating, or had started six or more ventures—the great majority felt they would have been pleased and surprised on gazing into that crystal ball in 1949. Of the men who had worked for only one employer or launched only one venture, disproportionately many put themselves down as unimpressed or disappointed.

This correlation must be read with care, of course. It cannot be stated as a general truth that frequent job-hopping leads to good luck—or, conversely, that it is categorically a bad idea to marry a single company and stay there throughout one's working life. As we will see, it all depends on how the job-hopping is conducted. Nor can it be said categorically that all men and women who have held many jobs or started many ventures are, by that criterion alone, bold.

Obviously none of the Forty-niners who put themselves in the pleased-surprised group had been badly kicked around by the world. Each felt that his frequent career moves had carried him upward toward personal goals—or at least that the last move had. Thus it can be said that these men's moves were generally conducted in the right way to produce lucky outcomes.

Conducted how? Boldly. The lucky Forty-niners were lucky at least partly because they had not been afraid to take risks in their lives—in some cases to take risks very frequently. That statement, taken alone, may make it sound as though these lucky men were mere gamblers who chanced to win. But the statement must not be taken alone. For there are many different kinds of risk-taking: the two main kinds are the smart and the dumb. Boldness is important to good luck, but it must be boldness of the right kind—boldness held in check by certain other internal mechanisms. Most of those pleased-surprised men had, in fact, displayed boldness of just that kind.

As a Forty-niner in good standing and as the class scribe, I have talked to many of the men about that questionnaire since it was conducted. I have also talked to other observers of life, luck, and character. It turns out that the old Latin bromide about fortune and the bold is true—if you read it carefully.

The First Rule: Be Eternally Ready to Inspect Lucky Opportunities When They Drift into View

"When I first got out of college," says one of the lucky Forty-niners, "I was full of those old Work Ethic teachings—you know, keep plugging along in a straight line, keep your nose to the grindstone, keep scrambling up the same damned mountain no matter how many times you slide down. But around age thirty I suddenly realized that the Work Ethic is a prescription for bad luck—or at least for throwing away good luck. The luckiest people I know haven't lived their lives in a straight line but in a zigzag. It's a mistake to get stuck on one track. You've got to be ready to jump off in a new direction when you see something good."

This man, after serving in the air force during the Korean War, joined a giant manufacturing company as a sales-management trainee. "There were thousands of us young guys in various parts of the company, all struggling up the pyramid. With each step up, the number of good spots got smaller, so it was obvious most of us were going to get shoved sideways into dead-end jobs before it all ended. But I had all those

ideas about grindstones and 'winners never quit' and all
that—and also there was the security, which was nice.
So for a long time I stuck with it, went in a straight
line."

Then an intriguing opportunity appeared mysteri-
ously on his horizon. In a Southern city on a sales trip,
he walked into a hotel dining room and saw an old
high-school friend at a table, eating alone. The friend
turned out to be in the business of selling mutual-fund
shares. In those days that was an obscure, quiet
business, but it was starting to grow rapidly. "My
friend was happy and prosperous. He told me his outfit
was anxious to hire new people and make them rich. I
was fascinated by what he told me of the business. It
was scary to think of leaving my secure job and starting something completely new, something I'd never
even thought of. But I told myself, 'See here, buddy,
luck has dealt you a wild card for free. Are you going
to throw it away because you're scared of it?' So in the
end I played it."

The mutual-fund business made him rich. He
worked for two companies over a period of several
years. Then a new opportunity drifted into view and he
jumped off in a different direction. He and two friends
opened their own investment-management company. It
prospered and so did he. Then came still another
chance. Through some of his contacts in the financial
world he was asked to join a state government commis-
sion that was being set up to study some of the state's
money problems. "I'd always wanted to get into government service, so I said okay. And right now I'm
looking at another exciting, scary opportunity. Last
month some people in my home city asked me to run
for mayor next year. I was tempted to say, 'No, I'm
not a politician,' but I didn't. I've learned my lesson. If
I'd said, 'No, I'm not a mutual-fund salesman' years
back I wouldn't be anywhere today. I'm a confirmed
zigzagger. It makes life exciting and rewarding. So next
year, maybe I'm going to be a politician."

"Audentes Fortuna Juvat"

One of the unluckier Forty-niners, on hearing the would-be mayor's story from me, nodded sadly over his third martini. The clear, still liquid in the glass looked as though it might have been his tears. "Today I know you've got to have the guts to make changes," he said. "I wish I'd known it when I was younger. But I was too comfortable where I was. My wife and I were both scared to pack up and try some new route. I got myself stuck. I mean really stuck. . . ."

He joined a department-store chain after graduation, stayed with the company for two decades, and got dead-ended as manager of one of its less active stores. The chain ran into severe trouble during the recession of the early 1970s and the store was closed. When I last saw the manager he was desperately hunting for a new job at the age of nearly fifty. His wife had found a job of her own and then, partly because his unhappiness was making him too hard to live with, had left him.

He sat in a bar with me and played the game of "if only," probably the saddest game on earth. "If only I'd had the guts to zigzag," he said, picking up the would-be mayor's terminology. He recalled that several attractive chances had drifted past him during his life. In one case a chance meeting on a fishing trip led him into contact with a business group that planned to build a marina. Boats had been his hobby since boyhood, and the group asked him if he would be interested in becoming the marina's manager, with a share in the profits and a chance to become a stockholder. But he had blinders on and could only see straight ahead. He had rigidly typecast himself as "manager of a retail store." The opportunity was off his main route, so he walked past it without inspecting it. "The guy who did take on the marina job is not only rich today, but he's doing what he loves to do and what I'd love to be doing. Ah, why was I so timid?"

"Luck comes to the mind prepared," says another of those hoary aphorisms. To put it another way, little bits of potential luck drift past nearly everybody from time to time. But they are only of value to those bold enough to reach out and grasp them.

Dr. Charles Cardwell is a philosophy professor at the Virginia Polytechnic Institute who has pondered the role of luck in life. He suggests that a distinction be made between the words "luck" and "fortune." Dr. Cardwell says: "You hear it said that people make their own luck. But if you take 'luck' to mean chance events, happenstance, then the statement isn't true. Luck happens to everybody. You don't make your own luck. It comes and goes on its own. But you *can* make your own fortune, by staying alert and using luck wisely."

By using it boldly, among other things. The store manager, by his own admission, failed to do this and lost the game. Perhaps his timidity stemmed from a failure to grasp the Second Rule clearly enough.

The Second Rule: Know the Difference Between Boldness and Rashness

If you bet your life savings on a spectacular venture in which you stand to lose everything, that is rash. If you accept an exciting new job opportunity even though it isn't on your straight-line route, even though you are scared by the thought of stepping into the unknown, that is bold.

In the speculative venture you may have much to gain, but you also have a fearsome amount to lose. In the case of the job there is also much to gain, but there is probably little to lose. Unnecessary timidity often comes from failing to make this distinction.

"What can you really lose when you jump into a new career?" asks another of the luckier Forty-niners. Luck came knocking at this man's door when he was past age forty. He left a "depressingly boring" executive job to start an entirely new career as a college teacher—something he had long wanted to do. "My wife and kids and I were all nervous and worried when this big chance suddenly came from out of the blue. But I asked myself, what am I really scared of? Moving into a new environment? Meeting new people? Making mistakes while learning new skills? Sure, I was scared of all those things and more. But I told my wife, 'Look, these things aren't matters of life and death. Even if everything goes wrong, we won't vanish off the face of the earth. We'll still be alive, we'll still have a house to live in and money for food. The risks we're taking aren't all that big. If this venture flops, I'll just go back to being an executive.' "

This man went so far as to imagine, in detail, the worst possible outcome of his venture. He then studied that outcome from various angles and concluded that it was not frightening enough to be a deterrent. "It turned out to be mostly nightmare—not real, not worth worrying about. The scenario went like this: One, my new teaching career doesn't work out. Two, I quit or get fired. Three, I try to pick up my executive career again. But, four, I'm in my forties or fifties and nobody wants to hire me."

To find whether this worst outcome was as frightening as it seemed, he talked to other men and women who had job-hunted when past forty. He even visited one of the Forty-Plus Clubs, which exist in many cities and are in business specifically to combat age discrimination in hiring. He came away optimistic.

"The message I got was: 'We won't promise you a rose garden. Finding an executive-level job at age forty-plus isn't easy. But guys do it every day. So do women, and they're up against sex discrimination as well as age. If you have good qualifications and really try, you can guess you'll be hired within three months of sending out your first batch of résumés. Six months would be unusually long.' "

Thus the very worst outcome to be expected was a period of six harried months without a salary. Was this so fearsome a fate? Was it dangerous enough to turn a bold move into a rash gamble? The man decided it was not. He concluded that his projected move into the academic world, while offering him enormous potential gains in personal growth and satisfaction, held only a minor degree of risk.

And so he grasped the chance and moved. The move cannot be called rash. It was only bold.

"Men and women who call themselves unlucky are often notably passive people," says psychiatrist Dr. Abraham Weinberg, who has spent years studying differences between the lucky and unlucky. "They tend to let life happen to them instead of using its opportunities in an assertive way. Often they are afraid of change itself, even change without risk. They tell themselves, 'I'm afraid of going into this new situation,' even when the situation holds no objective terrors except its newness. Instead of examining the situation and finding what the risks actually are, they simply drop out by saying, 'No, it's too much of a gamble.' It may not be a gamble at all. They are only making an excuse for staying in some familiar territory."

It is very easy to talk yourself out of a scary and challenging venture by calling it "rash." That one short word gives you a wonderful excuse for not doing anything—an excuse that may be almost unassailable. It has a sensible sound, a sound of reliable old folk wisdom. "Take no chances and you won't get hurt." You probably won't—but you may not cover much distance toward your personal goals either.

If you want to improve your luck, it is essential to study this distinction between the rash and the bold. Badger yourself about it. Force yourself to appraise situations honestly when they frighten you. It may turn out that you have been using "rash" as an excuse to avoid taking minor chances.

It is true that when we take chances, we stand to lose. But it is also true that we will never win anything if we never even enter the game. Lucky people are aware of the possibility of losing, and indeed they may lose often. But since the chances they take are small, the losses tend to be small. By being willing to accept small losses, they put themselves in position to make large gains.

Successful speculators and gamblers know this lesson well. An ancient piece of counsel often heard around gambling casinos and on Wall Street is: "Never gamble with grocery money." To speculate with money you need, funds that should be reserved for essentials of living, is obviously rash. (Also, it makes you too nervous to gamble cleverly.) But it is not necessarily rash to speculate with money that you can afford to lose— money whose loss, while perhaps painful, would not be tragic. That is bold. It can also be fun.

Perhaps gambling and speculation don't appeal to you. That is a matter of personal choice. But if you never buy a state lottery ticket or take a plunge in the stock market, you have no right to be jealous of somebody who does and wins. You have no right to grumble, "Some people have all the luck. Nothing like that ever happens to me." It doesn't happen because you have never entered the game.

Fortune favors neither the timid nor the rash. (The rash, however, do get a lot of exciting rides for their money.) Fortune favors the bold because they operate from a firm middle ground between the two extremes. They are not afraid to move once they determine that the odds are solidly on their side.

The Third Rule: Don't Insist on Having Total Advance Knowledge of Any Situation You Are About to Enter

J. Paul Getty, the oil billionaire who died in 1976, was a man who believed firmly in all three of the rules we have studied here—especially this last rule. It will be useful to look briefly at the life of this supremely lucky man. Getty was not only lucky but, until his last years, gregarious, enthusiastic, and articulate. He enjoyed dissecting his remarkable life to see what lessons it might embody for younger men and women just starting the long climb. I talked to him only once, but the vigor of his personality made a lasting impression on me.

It is widely believed that Getty's enormous fortune grew out of a lesser fortune inherited from his father, a lawyer-turned-oilman. That is not so. Getty's father did indeed die a millionaire, but by then J. Paul was a millionaire himself. He had made it on his own—at least partly by knowing how to be lucky.

In his early years he zigzagged, as lucky people so often do. He went to college thinking he wanted to be a writer. (Much later in his life he became a part-time one, and not a bad one at that.) Then he became interested in his own knack of dealing with people and decided he wanted to enter the U.S. diplomatic service. Out of college and about to look for his first government job, he found himself attracted by the Oklahoma oil boom in which his father was then enriching (and hugely enjoying) himself. The oil business was off young Getty's main route, but being of the lucky breed he felt compelled to grasp a chance boldly when it drifted by. He decided to postpone his diplomatic career for a year or so and try his hand as a wildcatter.

He raised money by working around other wildcatters' rigs and occasionally by borrowing from his father. His father, whose stern principles forbade coddling a son, never gave the young man any but trivial cash gifts and demanded prompt repayment of every borrowed nickel. Luckily young Getty was well aware of the difference between boldness and rashness. He never entered a venture whose cash requirements, in the event of a loss, were big enough to cause him serious hardship. Instead, he kept the cash needs low by depending on his talents as a smooth, canny, psychology-wise bargainer and salesman.

His first few ventures were flops. He began to think

about starting his diplomatic career. But early in 1916, drilling on a lease that he had secured at the bargain price of $500, he sank his first major producing well. It pumped some 700 barrels a day and founded the young man's fortune. (He was then but twenty-three.)

Lucky? Of course. But he deserved to be lucky. He had done everything right.

Later in his life people asked him where he found the nerve to risk $500 on that lucky lease. How did he know the well would produce? His answer was that he didn't know. He gathered all the facts he could, studied the site and the surrounding landscape, talked to geologists and other experts. He ended with a strong hunch that the spot was a good one. "But as for actually *knowing* what the outcome would be," he said, "that was impossible. If there were a way to be a hundred-percent sure where rich oil deposits are, nobody would ever sink a dry well. Oil prospecting is like any other venture in life, from getting married to buying a car. There is always an element of chance, and you must be willing to live with that element. If you insist on perfect certainty, you will never be able to make any decisions at all. You will simply paralyze yourself."

Getty had nothing against facts. His point was that, in almost any venture, there comes a time when you must stop gathering facts and boldly make a decision to go or not go. There seldom are quite enough facts. You seldom know everything you could wish to know. It makes perfectly good sense to inform yourself about a situation as well as you reasonably can, but there is always a point beyond which further fact-finding brings diminishing returns. If you pass that point and still take no action, still go on saying, "I'm studying it . . . I'm checking it out," you may only be making an excuse for timidity—another excuse like "rash." As Getty put it, you then become "like one of those government commissions that are afraid to make a decision. They hold hearings, collect facts, stew and fuss and keep very, very busy for months and months. After a while you know it's just a sham. The appearance of action is just a front to hide inaction."

Almost anything you can do to avoid this paralysis of endless fussing will help you. This is why it won't necessarily do you any harm and may be tangibly useful if you hold a mystical or occult belief—what others might call a "superstition."

In all modern industrial nations, of course, it is fashionable to deride superstitious ideas. This derision is an admired intellectual pose, from Moscow to Los Angeles. The so-called Age of Aquarius, which supposedly dawned in the 1960s, is said to be making people more tolerant of mystical and occult notions—but if it is, the increase in tolerance so far seems confined to certain rather small segments of the society. In most places it is not a good idea to admit that you believe in astrology or read Tarot cards, unless you grin while speaking to show you know you're dumb. But perhaps such beliefs are not so silly after all. Let's look at the practical uses of superstition.

A note on semantics. We've noted before that what is religion to one person may be superstition to another. The word "superstition" has derision built in. It means "an occult or mystical belief held by the ignorant"—or, to put it another way, "any belief other than my own." I don't like the word because of its sneer, but I must use it for lack of a convenient substitute. As used in this book it is to be understood with its sneer wiped off. Here it means simply "an occult or mystical belief not shared by everybody."

When I began talking to the lucky and unlucky many years ago, a puzzling fact became apparent to me very quickly. With exceptions, spectacularly lucky people are superstitious. Getty was among them. "Yes, I have a tidy little superstition," he told me when I asked him, though he offered no details. Leonard Bernstein has a pair of lucky cufflinks that he invariably wears when conducting. Truman Capote grows uncomfortable when he sees an ashtray with more than three cigarette butts in it and spends considerable energy keeping ashtrays emptied. Arlene Francis always wears a certain pendant when appearing before an audience, and if it doesn't go with her costume, she wears it concealed. With Zsa Zsa Gabor it's a ring given to her as a child.

A list of famous astrology buffs would fill a fair-sized telephone directory. President Grover Cleveland consulted an astrologer regularly. So did J. Pierpont Morgan. So did at least two presidents of the New York Stock Exchange, Jacob Stout and Seymour Cromwell. Cornelius ("Commodore") Vanderbilt was interested not only in the stars but also in ghosts. He consulted spirit mediums, who raised ghosts from whom Vanderbilt got tips about the future.

The apparently high incidence of superstitious ideas among successful men and women can be interpreted in at least two ways.

It can be used, and of course has been, to prove that a given approach works. "If astrology could do all that for J. Pierpont Morgan, think what it could do for you."

But the other interpretation does not ask you to believe that unseen forces are at work. Think of a superstition simply as a neat psychological device that can come to your aid in moments of worry, confusion, and indecision. In a situation where you must make a choice but are intimidated by the shortage of facts, a good, friendly superstition helps you avoid paralysis. When you have done all your homework, when you have diligently gathered all the essential facts of the situation, and when you still don't know what course to take because the available facts aren't enough, then a superstition is something to fall back on. It can relieve you from worrying and fussing over a choice that can't be improved by worrying and fussing. It helps make you bold.

Seen in this light, the high incidence of superstition among the lucky becomes easier to explain. Lucky people are lucky because, among other things, they often instinctively use superstitions to embolden themselves, make themselves more decisive. Like Getty, they know that there is an element of chance in nearly every venture, often a large element. That element is not amenable to any rational attack. No amount of fact-finding, no amount of figuring-out will change the odds or affect the outcome. This is where a superstition can make itself useful. It helps you make a choice quickly and relatively painlessly in the face of inadequate data.

We often come up against situations in which any choice could be wrong, but paralysis would be wronger. Frank Stockton's notorious, unfinished story about the lady and the tiger is an annoyingly memorable example. The hero of the story incurs the wrath of a king, who sentences him to make a difficult choice. He is locked in an arena from which the only exits are closed doors. Behind one is a lady; behind the other, a tiger who hasn't been eating regularly. The hero's attempts to make his choice rationally, with facts, only lead him into deeper confusion and indecision. He isn't helped when the princess, his lover, points to one of the doors, for he doesn't know whether she is motivated by sympathy or jealousy. Yet he *must* make a choice, for to stay in the arena without opening a door means a slow but certain death by starvation.

Stockton does not tell us what his hero did. One can hope for the hero's sake, however, that he harbored a superstition. Any superstition would have served. He was in a situation where no amount of fussing could help him to a wise choice—a situation in which his best move was to make a decision boldly and fast and be done with it. Perhaps he carried a lucky coin in his pocket. If he had tossed it, his troubles would have been over quickly.

Life often gives us closed-door problems like that. In a suburban Connecticut town recently a little girl failed to come home for supper. Her frantic parents and worried neighbors exhausted all rational attempts to find her—checked with her friends, phoned the school and the local candy store, and so on. When all these attempts failed, they knew they had a problem that could not be figured out intellectually. The little girl could have wandered off in any direction. There was absolutely no rational basis for deciding where to conduct the search.

The searchers might simply have sat down, paralyzed. Luckily a superstition came to their aid. One of the neighbor women had a half-serious hobby of telling fortunes with Tarot cards. The desperate parents went to her. She spread the cards out, studied them, and said they gave her "an impression of falling water, with stone around." Somebody thought of a nearby wooded park in which there was a small artificial waterfall. The searchers went there and eventually found the little girl lost in the woods.

Lucky? Of course. Magical? Maybe, maybe not. But whether or not you believe the Tarot cards actually knew where the lost child was, you must at least credit the superstition with forestalling paralysis. It got some action going. In that situation, inaction was the worst possible response. Many of the neighbors and police searchers that night thought the superstition was dumb, and perhaps it was. But it did get them up off their rumps and out into the night. The little girl would not have been found if they hadn't started to look *somewhere*.

Thus, if you harbor a superstition, treat it as a friend. Laugh at it in public if you like, but cherish it in private. It will help you decide which door to open. It will come to your aid if you are offered two jobs that seem equally attractive on the basis of available facts. Or if you think you are in love with two different people and want to marry both. Or if you can't decide where to go on vacation.

A friendly superstition not only helps you make choices in fact-short situations. It can also enhance your general feelings of confidence and competence—which are both components of boldness. A common superstition among bridge players, for instance, holds that you can change your luck by changing your seat. If you and your partner have been sitting east-west, you change to north-south and thus supposedly improve your chance of winning. Silly? Well, perhaps. But Charles Goren, for one, doesn't think so.

In his monthly *McCall's* column some years ago, Goren pointed out that you play better when you feel better. If changing your seat makes you feel better—luckier, more confident—the likelihood is that it will improve your play. You grow bolder, sharper, more decisive, more adept at seizing attractive chances. The change in seat actually changes your luck.

By contrast, it is usually not a good idea to argue with a cherished superstition. Helen Wills, a world-famous tennis player of the 1920s, held a nearly lifelong belief that it would be bad luck to put on her right shoe before the left one. She often ridiculed her own superstition. One day she determined to show it who was boss. She put on her right shoe first, went out to play tennis, and lost miserably.

"I just didn't feel right," she reported later. "I felt uncomfortable, couldn't concentrate . . . I know it's silly, but I'm not going to fight this thing anymore. From now on it's the left shoe first." And why not? The worst you could say about Helen Wills's superstition would be that it was harmless. The best would be that it boosted her feelings of confidence and competence. Though she herself often felt she was foolish to cherish it, she would have been still more foolish to defy it.

A superstition isn't likely to be harmful unless you use it *in place* of rational processes. It should come into play only when you have done your best to solve the problem or make the decision with straightforward thinking and hunching and plain hard work. It takes over where your own efforts end. An ancient piece of counsel assures us that "God helps those who help themselves." The same can be said for any mystical or occult power you call on.

"It is typical of chronic losers in the gambling world that they lean too heavily on magical solutions to their problems," says Dr. Jay Livingston, psychologist at Montclair (New Jersey) State College. He spent two years living with Gamblers Anonymous members and their families, trying to find out why some people are chronically unlucky and why they keep going back to get knocked down again. "The loser often has little faith in his own ability to get good results, so he depends on mysterious magical forces to see him through life. The mysterious forces won't usually do what he wants, of course.

"The winner is quite different. He may have superstitious ideas too, but he doesn't depend on magic to do *his* part of the job. For instance, take a baseball player on a hitting streak. He may believe it will be bad luck to change his socks, so he doesn't change them and that makes him feel good. But he still takes batting practice."

4.

The Ratchet Effect

A RATCHET IS a device that preserves gains. It allows a wheel to turn forward but prevents it from slipping backward.

Lucky people typically seem to organize their lives in an analogous way. They know that almost any venture can lead to either loss or gain. At the outset it is impossible to know which way the wheel will turn. But if it starts to turn the wrong way, the lucky are prepared to stop it. They have the capacity to get out of deteriorating situations quickly. They know how to discard bad luck before it becomes worse luck.

This sounds like a simple trick—little more, one might think, than plain common sense. But it evidently is not nearly as simple as it sounds. Great numbers of people—the essentially unlucky—never seem to master it. They habitually get themselves stuck in bad situations, in many cases stuck for life.

If the ratchet effect seems simple to understand, why can't everybody practice it successfully? It turns out that, for many, and perhaps the majority, two great emotional obstacles stand in the way.

These obstacles are not so big that they can't be overcome. Some men and women appear to overcome them fairly easily—which is one reason why we call those people lucky. The rest of us must work harder. The mere act of finding where those obstacles stand and studying their shape, however, quickly renders them less formidable. To know an opponent well is the first step in beating him. If you develop a clear understanding of some reasons why good luck has eluded you, you are already luckier than you were when you just sat around baffled, wailing, "Some people have all the luck!"

Let's study the two obstacles and see what can be done about climbing over them.

The First Obstacle: It's Too Hard to Say "I Was Wrong"

Gerald M. Loeb, who died in 1975, was a stock-market speculator—by all measures one of the brightest and luckiest to appear on Wall Street in recent times. Unlike many other bright stars who shone there in the booming 1950s and 1960s, Loeb and his money did not vanish when the long picnic ended in 1969. Nor did the money of those who listened to his counsel. For Loeb was a man who knew how to manage luck. In particular he understood the ratchet effect. He knew that the wheel wasn't always going to turn in this right direction, and when it started to slip backward, he was ready. He froze his luck where it stood. He got out of the market with most of his winnings intact.

Loeb was not only smart. He was also engagingly honest. His best-known book of advice was entitled *The Battle for Investment Survival.* I once asked him why he had given it that vaguely negative name, which made stock speculation sound like a lot of hard work and strife. Most other Wall Street how-to books promise huge profit, great fun, and hardly any work. Loeb agreed that his title was somewhat intimidating. He explained: "I don't want people coming up to me and saying, 'See here, Loeb, you said it would be easy but it wasn't.' The fact is, for most people this is one of the toughest ways on earth to make a dollar. Digging ditches is easier. My book has formulas that work, but they only work if you've got the guts to use them well. It takes discipline. It takes—it takes—I don't know, *something* that not everybody has."

One of the more important sections of the book was a formula for applying the ratchet effect to stock speculation. This formula was not original with Loeb. Wise old counselors were urging it on young hotbloods around Amsterdam's capital markets as far back as the sixteenth century. But Loeb expressed it more clearly and forcefully than most. He was able to do so because he had used the formula throughout his long risk-taking life (which began in 1920) and he had unequivocal faith in it. However, he knew as he wrote that relatively few of his readers would apply the formula boldly or decisively enough to make it work right. "On paper it looks perfectly logical," he mused gloomily. "People read it and say 'Hey! Yes! Terrific!' But when you actually start using it, you find it hurts. You find how much man or woman you are."

Essentially, the formula works like this. You select a stock to buy. Your selection is presumably based on diligent fact-gathering, smart advice, good hunching, and other elements of rational judgment. All the same, you must admit to yourself at the very start that you cannot know the future. If you have done your homework well, you have a reasonable basis for hoping your stock's price will rise to pleasing heights. But you cannot be sure. The price might start falling the day after you buy the stock, due to circumstances you could not foresee or combinations of facts that somehow didn't get mixed properly when you formed your hunch. Or the price might rise for a short while and then fall back. Or, if you are lucky, it won't fall until it has been climbing for a long time. None of this will be within your power to foresee or control. In stock speculation as in all human ventures, you are partly at the mercy of chance.

There is one certainty, however. Sooner or later, the price will drop. Whenever it does, in Loeb's formula, your ratchet mechanism goes into effect. You sell out whenever the price drops 10 to 15 percent from the highest level at which you have held the stock—*regardless of whether you then have a gain or a loss.*

Obviously this formula does not guarantee profits. You might buy several stocks in a row and watch in dismay as all of them drop 10 percent, forcing you to sell out. Anybody using the formula must be prepared to swallow a number of small losses while waiting for a gain. What the formula does guarantee is that you will never be smashed by a large loss, the kind that wiped out so many speculators in 1929 and 1969. The ratchet effect protects you against bad luck.

It is an entirely sensible formula. Unfortunately, relatively few people are able to use it successfully. As Loeb himself sadly pointed out, it hurts too much. For, among its other difficulties, it requires you to look yourself and other people in the eye once in a while and say, "I was wrong."

That smarts. Unbearably, sometimes. The typical small-time speculator avoids the pain and so remains a small-time speculator—or becomes a bankrupt one. If he buys a stock whose price begins to sag, he hangs on in the hope that future events will finally vindicate his judgment. "This price drop is just temporary," he tells himself hopefully. "I was right to buy the stock. It would be rash to sell out just because of some initial bad luck. If I sell, I'll be sorry. Time will show how smart I am."

It is perfectly true that he could be sorry if he sells. The Left-Behind Blues is one of Wall Street's saddest songs. It sings of the black gloom that enshrouds you when a stock you have just sold proceeds to double its price. This depressing experience can happen to anybody and does happen to thousands of morose traders every year. But there is absolutely no way to predict when it is going to happen. When a price begins to droop, it is wiser to guess it will continue to droop than to pray it will suddenly turn around. It is safer to take bold action and get out with a small loss.

Certainly you will be sad if your stock then takes off and leaves you behind. But you will be vastly sadder if you hang on and ride it down to oblivion.

This is what the unlucky speculator does too often, and it is one of the main reasons why he is unlucky. Emotionally unable to sell, he hangs onto his losers, praying that they will eventually climb back to the price at which he bought them. They may do that, months or years or decades later. (Many of 1969's losers are still losers—and for that matter so are some of 1929's.) If his losers return to their original price after ten years of waiting, he may be able to convince himself that he was smart after all. He will be able to say, "Aha! Now I don't have a loss anymore!" But his money will have been stuck in this stagnant investment for a decade, during which time he could have doubled it by storing it in long-term savings certificates. While his money was stuck, the luckier speculator had his money out doing useful work.

The lucky speculator, of course, probably had to live through several of those unpleasant experiences in which he said, "I was wrong." He had to admit it to himself, to his broker, to family members, perhaps to friends. It is entirely safe to assume he hated every minute of this mortification. But he determined that he had to go through it, and he did, boldly.

In an intriguing 1973 book, *Psyche, Sex and Stocks,* psychiatrist Stanley Block and psychologist Samuel Correnti reported on a long-term study of "born losers" in the market. One of the most common characteristics of this gloomy tribe, the two researchers determined, is "an overwhelming need to prove one's own brilliance." The need to feel and look smart undoubtedly exists in nearly every man and woman on earth. If it is well controlled, it can lead to admirable results. But if it becomes so overwhelming that it forbids you ever to admit you are wrong, even when all the factual evidence says plainly that you are, then the need becomes a cause of bad luck.

Its results are probably more clearly and directly visible on the stock market than anywhere else, but if you look hard enough you can see the same need causing trouble among the unlucky in almost all areas of life. You can see it in nearly any situation where the ratchet effect, quickly and boldly applied, could have rectified a bad decision—and where that quick and bold application never happened.

Dr. Ronald Raymond, a clinical psychologist who practices in Connecticut, finds that unlucky people often drift into marriages and other long-term relationships that they can guess won't work. Quick action in the beginning can end a flawed relationship before it becomes an entanglement, but that action, of course, requires somebody to say, "I was wrong." It may require one partner or both to go through the pain and embarrassment of calling off a wedding.

"People avoid doing that because they think it will make them seem dumb and ridiculous," Dr. Raymond says. "So even if they're starting to have serious doubts, they go on drifting toward the wedding day. The closer the day gets, the more entangled they get. Finally, by sheer inertia, they find themselves married without really wanting to be. And now they face years of unhappiness, maybe a lifetime of it. They end up consulting people like me, looking for a way out. What they should have done was to stand up before the wedding and say, 'Stop! I'm on the wrong train!' There is no sense in my telling them that. They already know it. But of course it's too late now."

The Luck Adjustment

It is often "too late" for the unlucky. There is almost always a time at the start of any souring venture when the ratchet effect can be applied fairly easily and you can get out with a minor loss or none. But that time may pass very quickly. After it has gone, the glue of circumstances rapidly hardens around your feet. You are stuck, perhaps for life.

"It's sad to think how many men and women are stuck in jobs they hate," says Bill Battalia, the executive recruiter. "In a lot of cases these are people who could have made changes earlier in their lives. But the longer you stay with a job or career, the tougher it is to quit."

F. Scott Fitzgerald was thinking of something like this when he said there are "no second acts in American lives." He exaggerated, of course. Men and women do sometimes change careers and redesign their lives in midstream. But this is so hard to do that it is not done often. It is certainly not a common pattern in America (or in Europe either, for that matter). In the common pattern, the main structural timbers of one's life are bolted in place by age thirty or earlier. Only minor tinkering takes place from then on.

If the structure turns out to be significantly less than the great soaring castle you once dreamed of, you will call yourself unlucky to one extent or another. The bad luck might have been avoided if you had been willing to say "I was wrong" before the main timbers were locked down.

Battalia tells a typical story of such avoidable bad luck. A young chemist left a small mining company in the Northwest to take a higher-paying job with a large company near New York City. His wife thought he was making a mistake. She was sure he would be miserable in an urban environment, away from his native mountains and trout streams. His boss, the president of the mining company, also thought the move unwise. The president doubted that the younger men would adapt well to life in a large organization. "My guess is that you'll be sitting here in my office within half a year, asking for your old job back," said the president, amiably. "I'll be waiting. When you want to come back, just let me know."

Within a few months of moving to the New York area, the young chemist knew his wife and his former boss were both right. He didn't like life in the metropolis. Moreover, a piece of unforeseeable bad luck developed in his new job. A management upheaval took place. The senior executive who had hired him, and who had promised to keep a broad avenue of growth possibilities open for him, was abruptly transferred to another part of the company and virtually stripped of power. When the upheaval was over, the chemist found that his job and future prospects were both quite different from what he had signed up for.

This would have been the time to put the ratchet mechanism into effect. But the chemist didn't want to tell his wife and former boss how right they had been. He stayed in New York and hoped the bad beginning would somehow evolve toward a happy ending.

"It's true that a problem will sometimes go away if you simply wait and do nothing," says Battalia. "I've known a lot of people who guide their lives by that philosophy. They think, 'If I just wait, maybe this person who is blocking me will go away. Maybe he'll die. Maybe this whole bad situation will change in some way I can't foresee.' Sure, problems do disappear once in a while if you give them time. But if you build a lifetime philosophy on this passive waiting idea, it seems to me you're bucking the odds. Problems don't usually go away—not fast, anyhow. More often, they stay there or get worse."

This is what happened to the chemist. By the time he finally determined that his problems weren't temporary, he was stuck. He might still have left that hard-luck job within the first few years, but the first obstacle wasn't all that stood in his way. He faced an-

other obstacle—and the longer he waited, the bigger it
grew.

The Second Obstacle: It's Too Hard to
Abandon an Investment

An investment may consist of money, love, time, effort, commitment, or a combination of any or all.
Whatever it is made of, it is a cherished thing, a thing
to be protected. If a venture of yours turns sour, the
only way you are going to get out of it is to abandon
what you have invested in it. That hurts at least as
much as admitting you were wrong. Much more, sometimes. It hurts some people so much that they seem unable to do it at all. Thus they get thoroughly trapped in
ill-fated ventures. They can only flounder helplessly as
bad luck turns to worse luck.

The chemist of Bill Battalia's story felt he had a
considerable investment in his New York job. There
was the initial cash investment: moving his family
across the country, buying and furnishing a house in
the suburbs. There was the investment of time, which
of course grew larger day by day. There was an enormous investment of effort, for the man had to work
hard to learn new skills for his job. He attended com-
pany-sponsored research seminars, enrolled in night
university courses to fill some gaps in his technical education. As the years rolled by, he also began to feel he
had an increasing investment in the company pension
and bonus plans, which both were designed to reward
long service.

After seven or eight years he felt trapped inextric-
ably behind this second obstacle. He now knew almost
for certain that the ideal job he had once dreamed of—
a job in pure research—was never going to materialize.
He was stuck in one of the company's least lively divi-
sions, in a job that mainly involved purchasing and
quality control. He is still there today, a middle-aged
man gloomily marking time until retirement. He is not a

happy man. He sometimes complains to friends that he didn't get the breaks other people got. This is true up to a point. But when his New York venture first started to turn sour, he could have applied the ratchet effect and walked out with no great loss. He could have gone away and looked for better breaks—if he had acted fast enough. He didn't. Too soon, it was too late.

This same reluctance to abandon an investment is the cause of much sorrow on Wall Street. The Loeb-style ratchet requires that you quickly and decisively abandon about a tenth of your money when bad luck strikes. You keep nine-tenths of it, which ought to be a comfort—but it is not comfort enough for many. The "constipated" investor, as Drs. Correnti and Block unkindly call him, can't bear to let anything go. Once he is in a venture, he is stuck in it even when it is plainly carrying him to his doom.

The obstacle can grow still more fearsome in gambling games such as poker. In a poker hand, as in many of life's more important ventures, you must keep adding to your investment if you want to stay in the game. In this respect poker is tougher than Wall Street. When you buy a stock (unless you buy on margin) you make a single investment and that is all. If the venture sours and if you don't get out, you are not required to do anything except watch miserably while your money shrinks. Nobody asks you to throw more money into the pot. Not so in poker. In that exquisitely agonizing game, you must continually invest new money to protect old money. The longer you stay in the pot, the bigger your investment grows and the more reluctant you are to abandon it.

Dr. E. Louis Mahigel, professor of communications at the University of Minnesota, is a man who knows much about poker and about the personalities of chronic losers and winners. He dropped out of high school at age fifteen and spent the next ten years earning his living as a professional gambler—"hustling," to use his own term. He made a good living at it.

He thinks his success came largely from the fact that he studied and understood people, "including myself." He finally tired of hustling, got his high-school equivalency diploma, went to college, and ended with a Ph.D. degree. But he still remembers all those poker games and the men and women who won and lost.

"An outstanding characteristic of the successful gambler, the pro," he says, "is that he knows how and when to get out of a hand and cut his losses. Of course he knows all the mathematical odds by heart, which gives him an edge over most people he hustles, but his main edge is in the area of emotion. When the odds say he probably won't win, he doesn't argue, he just leaves his money in the pot and lays down his cards. The chronic loser isn't emotionally equipped to do that. He's so desperate not to lose his investment that he takes wild chances to protect it."

The willingness to accept a string of small losses while waiting for a big gain: this is a key trait of all gamblers and speculators who succeed over a long term. *All* of them. It is also a key trait of lucky men and women in general. As Gerald Loeb put it, "Knowing when to sell out and having the guts to do it at the right time—this is an essential technique of successful living. It doesn't apply only to stock speculation. It is better to use the technique inefficiently than never learn it at all."

Lucky men and women do indeed have the capacity to sell out when they need to. They typically avoid getting trapped in unsatisfactory love relationships. They know it is better to get out of such a relationship before it hardens into a marriage, even if in doing so you must abandon an investment of love. They get out of bad job situations without waiting too long, even though it means leaving behind an investment of self.

I once met a Swiss banker and self-made millionaire who summed up his investment philosophy thus: "If you are losing a tug-of-war with a tiger, give him the rope before he gets to your arm. You can always buy a new rope." There are times in life when you must take a small loss to escape a big one. Probably almost everybody on earth older than ten, if questioned about this, would acknowledge its truth. But only the lucky seem able to act on it regularly.

Nothing that has been said in this chapter (or the previous one) should be interpreted to mean that the lucky as a breed are fickle or capricious. There is no evidence that you can improve your luck by bouncing at random from situation to situation, from person to person, from place to place like a golf ball shot into a forest. The useful reaction is to assess each situation and stay with it if it promises to produce the results you had hoped for. Only if it turns sour does the ratchet come into play.

Most lucky people whose lives I've studied have not been capricious in making their moves. They have not sought change for the sake of change itself—change prompted by chronic boredom or a childish hope that the grass would be greener behind the next fence. They have not job-hopped sideways, from one job to a similar job to yet another. Nor have they been multiple divorcees, stumbling in and out of personal commitments in a confused search for some unknown private bliss. A state of continual, restless, aimless bouncing doesn't demonstrably increase the odds of finding good luck and indeed may lead directly to bad luck in some cases.

As far as luck is concerned, there seem to be only two useful reasons for making a change. We discussed one in the previous chapter: a piece of clearly defined good luck has drifted into view and you boldly seize it. In this chapter we looked at the other: a situation has gone wrong—bad luck has appeared—and you apply the ratchet and get out, quickly, before things go wronger and before you are stuck.

Boldness and the ratchet effect are twin components of the luck adjustment. Within limits, they enable you to select your own luck. You seize the good and discard the bad. It might be almost like picking apples from a barrel, except that it is much, much harder to do. It is so much harder that only a minority of men and women know how. We call them lucky.

Notice one last thing about boldness and the ratchet effect. They complement each other. If you are bold, your ratchet mechanism is likely to work fast and decisively when you need it. And if your ratchet is working reliably—if you have confidence that it won't leave you stuck in wrong places—that fact can support your boldness.

With a ratchet that works, you can enter attractive ventures that might otherwise have scared you away. You tell yourself, "Yes, in this venture I stand to lose something if my luck turns bad. But I won't let myself lose much. If this job doesn't pan out, if I don't get along with this person, if the stock market slumps tomorrow . . . I'll admit I was wrong, leave 10 percent behind and pull out."

And so you are into the venture, boldly. Your potential losses are limited, but your potential gains aren't. Within limits, but in a perfectly real way, your luck is under your own control.

5.

The Pessimism Paradox

THE WORDS "LUCKY" and "optimistic" are somehow thought to belong together. When I began buttonholing lucky and unlucky people years ago I expected to find that the luckiest would be overwhelmingly optimistic. I was wrong.

Lucky people are generally happy, of course. We call them lucky and they so consider themselves because, partly through their own efforts and partly through the workings of chance (or fate or God or something else) they have reached personal goals that are important to them. It is accurate to call most of them pleased, contented, satisfied. They grin a lot. They are fun to be with. But to call them optimistic is to misuse the word. To be optimistic is to expect the best results. Lucky people, as a rule, don't. In fact the majority of them nurture a basic core of pessimism so dense and tough and prickly that it startles you when you first come upon it. Yes: *nurture*. They tend their pessimism with loving care, guard it against assaults, exercise it daily to keep it lean and hard. Sometimes consciously and sometimes intuitively, they cherish it as a thing of value. To lose it would be to lose—well, luck.

It was hard for me to come to grips with this phenomenon at first. It seemed paradoxical. Shouldn't lucky men and women be optimistic? It puzzled me to hear a professional Las Vegas gambler say, "Don't think about winning until you've made yourself ready to lose." Or to hear J. Paul Getty say, "When I go into any business deal, my chief thoughts are on how I'm going to save myself if things go wrong." Or to hear a brilliantly successful woman commodities speculator say, "Out of every four trades, I figure I'll lose money on three. And I'm not surprised when I lose on all four."

Canny old Gerald Loeb said it in a way that startled me the most. "On the stock market," he said flatly, "optimism can kill you."

We had better find out what is going on.

It turns out that the uses of pessimism among the lucky can be articulated in terms of two cardinal laws. These laws interlock. They should be thought of together, for they are really two parts of one law. For clarity, however, let's separate them temporarily and study them one by one.

Murphy's Law

As far as I have been able to discover, there is not now and has never been a Professor Murphy, originator of Murphy's Law. The reasons why this particular name is associated with this law are lost in the mists of time. The law, however, is well known and often reiterated among engineers, business people, and others who crave certainty in an uncertain world. The law says, "If something can go wrong, it will."

In a previous chapter we saw that fortune favors the

bold, and we studied some reasons why boldness increases the chances of finding good luck. But we also saw that lucky people go into every venture equipped with a ratchet mechanism, just in case things go wrong. Lucky people are by definition people whom fortune has favored—but one reason why they are favored is that they never assume they will be. They know Fortuna is fickle. She caresses you fondly today, perhaps. Tomorrow she may kick you.

Never, never assume you are fortune's darling. Just when life is at its best and brightest, just when you seem to be lifted up and nourished and protected by unassailable good luck—that is when you are most vulnerable to bad luck. That is when euphoria can melt your pessimism. When pessimism goes, you are in a state of peril. Your guard drops. You disconnect your ratchet mechanism. You disregard odd little hunches that are trying to tell you what you don't want to hear. And then, suddenly, you are face-down in the mud with fortune's foot on your neck.

Helena Rubinstein, who made her fortune in a world that was not hospitable to women in business, understood Murphy's Law unusually well. She was gifted with a rock-hard pessimism that no euphoria could melt. Shortly before her death at age ninety-five she wrote a book, *My Life for Beauty*, in which she described the stunning growth of her enterprise from a walkup beauty salon in Australia to a renowned international corporation. She freely acknowledged the mysterious role of luck. The book is full of phrases like "twist of fate" and "angel of luck." Unfortunately she said little about the causes behind all that luck, and in an apparent attempt to maintain a lighthearted tone she said almost nothing about what I take to be one of her key traits: that granite block of pessimism.

Pessimism? Indeed. I phoned her once on a magazine assignment, and as soon as she found I was calling from a booth she insisted that I give her my number, "in case we're cut off." The possibility had not occurred to me, but this was evidently a woman who knew Murphy's Law thoroughly. If something can go wrong, it will. It did. We *were* cut off, and I found my pockets empty of coins.

Pessimism had, of course, served her in vastly more important ways during her lucky and eventful life. Her own version of Murphy's Law was: "If there is a wrong way to use this product, somebody will find it." And the corollary: "The woman who finds it will have friends who talk a lot." Once, when a new skin cream was under development, she asked what would happen if somebody left a jar of it on a radiator. What happened was potential commercial disaster. The product, when warmed, turned into a loathsome, scummy soap. It was abandoned.

In London she met and admired Isadora Duncan, the dancer. Helena Rubenstein had always been attracted by what she called "flair" in both interior decoration and clothing—the dramatic, the colorful—and she was fascinated by the long, trailing scarves and shawls that the dancer habitually wore. "I wondered how they would look on me," she reported later. But as a student of Murphy's Law she eventually rejected the thought. She imagined the scarves getting caught in closing doors, falling into soup at dinner parties, pulling fragile statuettes off shelves. In this case her pessimism didn't go quite far enough. Isadora Duncan was killed at age forty-nine when the ends of her scarf got tangled in the wheel of a moving car.

Isadora Duncan may have belonged to that troubled tribe of people whom psychologists and family doctors call "accident-prone." Most of her accidents were trival—stubbed toes, cut fingers—but some were or could have been serious, as when she fell through a hole in the deck of a ship. These accidents evidently weren't caused by physical clumsiness or ineptitude, for she was a woman of extraordinary grace, at least when performing on a stage. The truth seems to be that Isadora Duncan was simply a woman who, when something could go wrong, allowed it to. Her carelessness, not only in terms of physical injury but in all areas of her life, was sometimes incredible. She had three illegitimate children (all of whom died before she did, one shortly after birth and two in an auto accident). She was eternally in trouble with various government agencies over lost passports and other documents. She was usually broke and spent much of her time scrambling away from angry creditors—not because of inadequate income but because of astoundingly bad management.

An old psychoanalytic theory held that a person such as this—continually in trouble despite a grand talent, plagued by accidents, finally dead too young—probably harbored a subconscious wish to destroy herself. The theory still has some currency among dinner-party analysts, but its acceptance among mental-health professionals is diminishing. Dr. Frederick I. McGuire, a University of California psychiatrist and nationally known authority on accident-proneness, views the theory with caution. "It is true that masochistic and suicidal feelings seem to be involved in some accidents," he says, "but to use that as a blanket explanation of accident-proneness in general would be wrong. There are many possible explanations."

Dr. Jay Livingston, the Montclair State College psychologist who has studied chronic losers among Gamblers Anonymous members, echoes Dr. McGuire's thought. "The old psychoanalytic view is outdated," he says. "Whether you're talking about accidents or any other variety of apparent, chronic bad luck, it isn't consistent with the facts as I know them to say that most or even many losers want to lose. Most men and women in my experience want to *win*. When they lose, it isn't because they want to but because of some other problem—in many cases, an oversupply of optimism."

Or, to put it in terms of Murphy's Law, an undersupply of pessimism. This seems to have been the chief factor in Isadora Duncan's astonishing life of accidents and lost documents and money troubles. She evidently trusted too much in luck. "I belong to the gods," she wrote in her rather pompous and windy autobiography. "My life is ruled by signs and portents. . . ." Entering each new situation, she expected that those gods (or to put it more simply, luck) would take care of her. She seldom stopped to ask what might go wrong or to take precautions against bad luck. Once, when she impulsively scheduled a large party and dancing exhibition outdoors, a friend suggested that it might be prudent to find an alternate indoor location in case of rain. She chided him for being "stuffy" and added dramatically, "Life is to be lived, not worried over!" It rained, of course. Among the few people who turned up was the caterer, demanding payment for a mountain of expensive foods that could not be stored.

This is part of the paradox. People who trust luck the most are among the least lucky. For Fortuna, when you lean against her too hard, often steps aside. Lucky people avoid accidents largely by being pessimistic. They ask, "What can go wrong when I paint the inside of this bedroom door? Of course! Even though I hang a sign on the other side, some nitwit will open the door at exactly the wrong moment. The door will hit me in the face. Or it will hit me in the elbow and make me drop my brush on the floor. Or it will knock over the paint can. Or all three. To insure my luck, I will behave as though all these things are certain to happen. I'll put the can there, not here, and I'll stand with my foot against the door. . . ." By contrast, the unlucky tend to shrug and say, "Oh, I'll trust to my luck. The odds are with me. It will only take me ten minutes to do the job. The kids aren't around, and Grandfather is taking his nap in front of the TV set. . . ." It can almost be predicted, of course, that this will be the one day of the year when Grandfather can't sleep and comes blundering through the door in search of his spectacles.

An exhaustive, years-long study of accidents among bus drivers, conducted in South Africa, reached similar conclusions about the importance of pessimism. Among "bad-risk" drivers—those who had been involved in more than a normal share of accidents—an outstanding personality trait turned out to be overoptimism. This optimism applied in three directions. The bad risk driver had too much faith in (1) his own skills, (2) other drivers' good sense and skills, and (3) luck. Some of the most accident-prone drivers were highly superstitious. They relied heavily on luck (which each, of course, defined in his own way) to see them through life and across dangerous traffic intersections, instead of trying to control their destinies themselves. We've seen before that a friendly superstition can be useful in certain decision-making situations—but only after all rational approaches to the given problem have been exhausted.

The problem of underdeveloped pessimism shows up in another group of chronic losers: that harassed tribe of men and women who are always hemorrhaging money at racetracks and gambling tables. The psychoanalytic theory about subconscious self-destructive urges has been applied to compulsive gamblers as well as to the accident-prone. I've remarked before that I have never found any factual support for the theory at any casino, track, or sidewalk craps game. It doesn't hold water, except perhaps in the cases of some very unusual, severely disturbed individuals. Almost all gamblers want good luck. Almost all are depressed when they lose. When they win, they often go into transports of exaggerated delight—and it is to seek this delight, this emotional orgasm, which for some is life's profoundest pleasure, that they repeatedly put their money in Fortuna's unreliable hands.

They harbor no wish to go broke and starve. Far from it. In most cases the problem is too much optimism. "If you look at the histories of compulsive gamblers," says Dr. Jay Livingston, "you often find that they are people who won early on. When they first started gambling, luck was good to them. They enjoyed the experience so much that they wanted it again and again. Of course they can't have it again and again. The laws of probability forbid it. You know that and I know it, but the compulsive gambler just goes on hoping."

The curse of optimism. Dr. William Boyd, the UCLA psychiatrist and devoted student of risk-taking, is another man who thinks "beginner's luck" can be dangerous. "If you have within you the seeds of whatever makes a compulsive gambler," he says, "the very best thing that could happen to you would be to lose miserably the first few times you bet. If the latent compulsive gambler happens to enjoy beginner's luck, that can be very bad luck indeed. It can be the person's doom."

And so it is with life as a whole. One way of looking at the insurance business is that it sells pessimism. You buy insurance to protect you against bad luck. If you don't expect bad luck—if you feel that the stars or your personal gods or some other mystical agency will protect you—you don't buy insurance. "As a general rule," says Peter Fagan, a Northwestern Mutual agent, "my toughest prospects are young adults who have enjoyed good luck in their early lives. Nothing bad has happened to them or to people in their families—no illness, no big money problems—so they feel invincible. Sometimes it's just a vague feeling, but sometimes they really believe some kind of favoritism is going on. They'll say, 'Oh, I've always been lucky,' or 'Whenever I'm in trouble, something always seems to turn up.' I always feel bad when I throw cold water on this kind of happy optimism, but the fact is, these very lucky people are the most vulnerable to bad luck. They don't buy insurance or take other precautions. Just because they feel lucky, they are the very ones who can get hit by catastrophic bad luck later on."

The condition of feeling lucky can be a condition of great personal danger. Never let the feeling take root. Never forget Murphy's Law.

Professional gamblers—the cool ones who win, as against the compulsive ones who lose—go further than that. To them, Murphy's Law is too mild. They don't merely expect something to go wrong. They expect it to go wrong in the worst possible way. They don't prepare just for average bad luck, but for outrageously bad luck.

"The losers," says one Las Vegas pro, "never do any thinking about the problem of 'strain,' as we call it. Strain means the demand on your gambling capital during a losing streak. You must have enough capital to absorb a string of losses while you're waiting for the breaks to come your way. The more capital you have, the more strain you can take. What the losers around here do is, they always underestimate the strain. They go into a game with much too short a supply of cash. They figure, 'Well, I've got plenty to see me through a run-of-the-mill losing streak.' Every pro knows that isn't the way things work. You've got to expect more than run-of-the-mill bad luck. You've got to be ready for *hellish* bad luck."

This truth can be illustrated simply with the romantic and maddening old game of roulette. Suppose you elect to play one of the even-money games, say red-black. You restrict yourself to a bet of one dollar on each coup. The law of averages, when inspected too casually, seems to say you should win roughly once in every two coups, with an occasional extra loss when the ivory ball falls into one of the green "house" numbers. You might tell yourself, "I know the colors won't come up red-black-red-black all night like a clock going tick-tock. There will be runs of one color and runs of the other. I'll prepare for bad luck and figure that there might be as many as five successive coups when I lose. Allowing an extra buck or two for the house numbers, I'll figure I can stand the strain by going into the game with seven dollars. With that, I can play all night!"

With that, you can easily be cleaned out by the tenth

or fifteenth coup—or, with worse luck, earlier. You simply have not allowed for your luck to get as bad as luck can get.

If it were not for this problem of strain, it would be easy to devise any number of foolproof systems for beating the wheel. To beat it, you would merely increase the size of your bet after each loss. You would bet enough so that an eventual win would allow you to recoup all your past losses. It sounds simple, but it would require astronomical amounts of capital in a long losing streak. (And just in case somebody with astronomical capital does come around, all casinos protect themselves by placing limits on the sizes of allowable bets.) Mainly for this reason, none of the dozens of roulette "winning systems" that have been devised over the centuries—and are still peddled to optimistic suckers in Las Vegas and Monte Carlo today—can work reliably. Some will work tolerably well if you have just average bad luck. None can work when you encounter what you are certain to encounter in the long run: worse-than-average bad luck.

Martin Gardner, the mathematical gamesman and disciple of randomness, is a firm adherent to this principle that we should be ready for the very worst to happen. In one of his *Scientific American* essays he quoted a man named Billy Lee, who wrote: "Don't worry, lightning never strikes in the same

Mitchell's Law

Martha Mitchell was born obscurely in Arkansas, battled her way to success as a model, married a fast-rising lawyer, climbed to a dizzy peak of fame and fortune, and then saw her life come apart piece by piece in the last inglorious days of the Nixon Administration. Two editors and I met her for lunch in New York one day in 1975. We wanted to talk about an autobiography that she thought she might write. Newspaper stories over the previous few years had prepared us to meet a woman of loud voice and large ego. We met no such woman. Martha Mitchell said softly, "Life is slippery like a piece of soap. If you think you have a good grip on it, you are wrong."

That is Mitchell's Law. I attach her name to it mainly to give it a name (and perhaps because I grew fond of her). Other names might have served as well, for other men and woman have articulated the law in their own words. Executive recruiter Bill Battalia, for instance: "People like to talk about planning their lives, but at least half the planning is done by luck or fate or whatever you want to call it. If a successful man comes up to me and says he planned his life just the way it turned out, I'll tell him he's suffering from a case of selective memory." Or Kirk Douglas: "We like to think we control our lives, but it's a damned illusion. There's always the X factor. . . ."

The X factor is luck. At the beginning of this book I defined luck as "events that influence our lives and are seemingly beyond our control." If you think you can make your life immune to such events, you are deluded. The delusion can be dangerous.

"There was a time when I had the world on a leash," Martha Mitchell said. "I had everything I wanted, and I also had a feeling of *control*. I felt I was in control of my life. I thought, 'As long as I'm careful, nothing can slip away from me now.' Well, the feeling was false. It all slipped away. There were precautions I could have taken, things I could have done, if only I hadn't felt so strong and confident. . . ."

She was saying that pessimism would have been useful—pessimism about her own degree of control over events. In the 1960s she could not have foreseen all that would happen to her: that her husband would become involved in a disastrous governmental scandal, that he and she would fall headlong from the high social-political mountaintop on which she thrived, that the two of them would part in the midst of the turmoil, and that she would be left lonely, powerless, sick, and virtually broke. Nobody could have predicted this bewildering sequence of events. But the possibility of bad luck could have been and should have been taken into account. Martha Mitchell could have taken precautions, at least in terms of money—and also in terms of her own emotions, so that the sudden appearance of ill fortune would not have been so surprising and devastating. At the height of her glory she could have said, "Life is slippery like a piece of soap." As she sadly admitted, she came to that realization too late.

Lucky men and women, notably more than the unlucky, are aware that unforeseeable and uncontrollable events may come blundering into their lives at any time. No life is ever totally under the control of its owner. Lucky people are those who adapt to this environment of uncertainty. They ready themselves for its opportunities, guard themselves against its hazards. If a piece of good luck drifts by—as we've seen—they seize it instead of ignoring it and continuing to plod forward in a straight line toward some planned goal. If bad luck comes, they are poised to jump aside quickly before it engulfs them. As a tribe, the lucky harbor no delusions that life is orderly, that it can be planned with precision, that it will happen exactly as one wishes. Its disorderliness pleases and excites some but irritates others, just as it irritates the unlucky. The difference is that the lucky accept the disorder as a fact that must be dealt with, whether they like it or not.

The unlucky tend to argue with it instead of accepting it. This was clearly illustrated in a study by Dr. Eugene Emerson Jennings, professor of administrative science at Michigan State University. He examined the lives of executives in an attempt to learn what qualities made for success or failure. In the remarkable book that came out of this years-long study, *Executive Success*, he reported that two outstanding traits of the "failure-prone" executive are an "illusion of immunity" to bad luck and an "illusion of mastery" over all of life's events.

"The executive's job is to make things happen by design," Professor Jennings wrote. "[But] occasionally things happen by error and chance." The consistently successful executive is emotionally prepared for such bad luck and is not demoralized when it strikes. The failure-prone executive, with his twin illusions of immunity and mastery, is likely to be knocked off balance.

"Each executive has a style of chance," says Dr. Jennings. The successful man or woman is aware that chance can make pulp out of the most carefully constructed plans. When that happens the successful executive is unhappy, of course, but can rise above the misfortune by saying, "Well, part of this was my own bad management, but part of it was sheer bad luck." The failure-prone executive is not emotionally equipped to handle random disaster in this serene way. Since he clings to the illusion that he has or should have total control over events, his tendency is to blame himself when bad luck steps in and takes things out of his hands. His reaction is: "I've failed."

Mathematician Horace Levinson feels this reaction causes a good deal of trouble in the business world, for its effect is to make bad luck worse. In *Chance, Luck and Statistics* Dr. Levinson postulates a situation in which a sales manager draws up a clever plan for snatching a share of the market from a competitor. On the plan's first trial, bad luck enters the picture and everything goes wrong. The sales manager wants to try again. He argues: "The plan was wrecked by chance events. Those events aren't likely to happen in the same way a second time." They *might* happen again, and any good pessimist would prepare defenses against them. But other people in the company don't want to try again. "Look at the facts," they say. "The plan failed." Thus a potential good idea is abandoned and maybe a good executive is hurt. The story, says Dr.

Levinson, illustrates "a type of thinking that is altogether too common in business. It consists in leaving out of account, either wholly or in part, the element of chance in business affairs."

Or in human affairs as a whole. If you cling to an illusion of control, you open yourself to two kinds of danger. The first danger is that you won't build defenses against the unknowable bad luck that at any hour could snatch control from your grasp. The second is that, when bad luck strikes, you will be too greatly demoralized. You will react in ways that are not useful.

Professional gamblers are smarter than many business people in this respect. In the words of Dr. Louis Mahigel, the former hustler turned college professor, "The pro knows that the results of a given card game will depend partly on luck and partly on skill. He is very, very careful to keep the two elements separate in his mind. He preys on suckers who, among their other problems, don't separate the two. Typically, the sucker thinks he has more control than he has."

If the sucker gets a string of good hands and amasses a pretty little pile of chips next to his elbow, he typically reacts in one of two ways. He thinks, "Wow, I'm smart!" Or he thinks, "Lady Luck is with me tonight! I can't lose!" Either way he develops an illusion of mastery, a feeling that events are somehow under his control.

The hustler across the table, observing this, grows happy. He knows, now, that the sucker can be induced to bet large amounts on hands that are not worth a nickel. The sucker is not prepared for the luck of the game to change. He believes his skill or luck or both make him invincible. The hustler will reinforce this fallacy with carefully planted comments: "That was smart betting! . . . Man, you're hot tonight!" The hustler has enough capital to take plenty of strain, and he waits patiently until good luck finally comes his way. Then he pounces. The sucker will lose everything he won, plus all his capital—plus, if the hustler works him well, everything he can borrow.

It is always a mistake to be sure of your own grip on events. Among the clearest expositions of this lesson was a fascinating but little-noted book published a few years ago: *The Loser*, by William S. Hoffman, Jr. Hoffman was a compulsive gambler—he was especially fond of horses—and the book is an account of his long, slow fall to the depths of poverty, debt, and degradation. He evidently violated almost every rule of the Luck Adjustment, including this last one, the one requiring pessimism. In particular he carried in his mind an old Work Ethic teaching that he had heard from his father, an athletic coach of some renown. The preachment said: "If you're good, you don't need luck."

We have noted before that some lessons of the Work Ethic are lessons in the cultivation of bad luck. This one is perhaps the worst. It is so obviously a fallacy that one wonders why it has survived so long. Hoffman, however, like many other unlucky people, apparently wove it tightly into his general philosophy of life. He believed he was good at playing the horses. He probably was good. Certainly he gave himself plenty of practice. But he had so much faith in his skill that he belittled the element of chance. It was a much bigger element than he was willing to admit. It did him in.

Never ignore that possibility of bad luck. It is always there. Doubt your own grip on events. Be prepared for them to slide from your grasp at any time, in any direction, with any result.

For Martha Mitchell was demonstrably right. Life is slippery like a piece of soap.

We have looked at Murphy's Law and Mitchell's Law separately. Now let's put them together and see what we have.

Murphy's Law counsels us not to depend too much on luck, for things are as likely to go wrong as right.

209

The Luck Adjustment

Mitchell's Law counsels us not to depend too much on our own control over events, for that control is less good than we sometimes like to think.

Both laws say: *Never enter a situation without knowing what you will do when it goes wrong.*

That is the pessimism of the lucky. Buried amid the pessimism, however, is a particular little piece of optimism. For if bad luck can wrench control from our grasp, so can good luck. We looked at this pleasing possibility in studying the *audentes fortuna juvat* phenomenon. The bold are ready to grab a piece of good luck when it drifts by, even if it means going off in a new, unplanned direction. They don't try to control their lives so rigidly that they ignore lucky breaks lying off the main track.

Thus the pessimistic laws of Murphy and Mitchell can be said to have this optimistic corollary: *If something goes right, don't argue.* Or to put it another way: *When good luck pulls you sideways, let go.*

You might as well. Life is slippery no matter how you handle it. Perfect control is an illusion. Good luck.

We know you don't read just one kind of book. | That's why we've got all kinds of bestsellers.

NEW FROM BALLANTINE!

FALCONER, John Cheever 27300 $2.25

The unforgettable story of a substantial, middle-class man and the passions that propel him into murder, prison, and an undreamed-of liberation. "CHEEVER'S TRIUMPH . . . A GREAT AMERICAN NOVEL."—*Newsweek*

GOODBYE, W. H. Manville 27118 $2.25

What happens when a woman turns a sexual fantasy into a fatal reality? The erotic thriller of the year! "Powerful."—*Village Voice.* "Hypnotic."—*Cosmopolitan.*

THE CAMERA NEVER BLINKS, Dan Rather
with Mickey Herskowitz 27423 $2.25

In this candid book, the co-editor of "60 Minutes" sketches vivid portraits of numerous personalities including JFK, LBJ and Nixon, and discusses his famous colleagues.

THE DRAGONS OF EDEN, Carl Sagan 26031 $2.25

An exciting and witty exploration of mankind's intelligence from pre-recorded time to the fantasy of a future race, by America's most appealing scientific spokesman.

VALENTINA, Fern Michaels 26011 $1.95

Sold into slavery in the Third Crusade, Valentina becomes a queen, only to find herself a slave to love.

THE BLACK DEATH, Gwyneth Cravens
and John S. Marr 27155 $2.50

A totally plausible novel of the panic that strikes when the bubonic plague devastates New York.

THE FLOWER OF THE STORM,
Beatrice Coogan 27368 $2.50

Love, pride and high drama set against the turbulent background of 19th century Ireland as a beautiful young woman fights for her inheritance and the man she loves.

THE JUDGMENT OF DEKE HUNTER,
George V. Higgins 25862 $1.95

Tough, dirty, shrewd, telling! "The best novel Higgins has written. Deke Hunter should have as many friends as Eddie Coyle."—*Kirkus Reviews*

LG-2